7 February 1998

McKenzie Clan,

Welcome to Aotearoa.

Trust your stay will be
enjoyable and you will return.

Helen
&
Brian

Discover
NEW
ZEALAND
The Glorious Islands

Discover
NEW
ZEALAND
The Glorious Islands

RAY JOYCE PHOTOGRAPHY   BILL SAUNDERS TEXT

cumulus

ACKNOWLEDGEMENTS
The author and photographer particularly wish to thank
Gavin Craig of Air Safaris Ltd, Noel Boyd of Helicopters (NZ) Ltd,
and Nelson Aero Club for their help in the
preparation of this book.

This edition published 1994 by
Whitcoulls Ltd, Private Bag 92098, Auckland, New Zealand

© Whitcoulls Ltd 1994

First published by Lansdowne Press/Beckett 1982

Designed by Elaine Rushbrooke
Computer photocomposed in Australia by Griffin Press Ltd
Printed in Hong Kong by South China Printing Co. (1988) Limited

Contents

Introduction 8

West Coast 10

Fiordland 30

Southland, Otago 48

Canterbury 70

Marlborough, Nelson 94

Bay of Plenty and East Cape   114

Hawkes Bay, Wairarapa   132

Wellington, Manawatu   152

Taranaki, King Country   164

The North   180

Index   204

Introduction

There was the seascape
Crammed with coast, surprising
As new lands will, the sailor
Moving on the face of the waters . . .
Landfall in Unknown Seas Allen Curnow

This little island country lay in the vast southern ocean, undisturbed by man until Polynesians landed a mere thousand or so years ago. Then three hundred years ago, European eyes first gazed upon 'the seascape crammed with coast'. After gaining a foothold on that coast, the invaders turned inland and began displacing the forest and birds with pasture and sheep. In the last century and a half the landscape has been transformed as New Zealanders sought their living from the soil of the new land. In their preoccupation with developing a farming economy their perception of the country has centred on its rural land. The national self-image has also focused on the extremes of its natural features—the glaciers and mountain peaks of the Southern Alps, the bubbling pools and geysers of the North Island's volcanic region. In the course of promoting Nature's aberrations to attract the tourist trade, as well as concentrating on their primary wealth, New Zealanders have overlooked the importance and beauties of their coastline.

The slim islands, reaching from subtropical to subantarctic waters, contain a remarkable diversity and length of coastline. Between the mangrove-fringed inlets of the north and the glaciated fiords of the south, there are at least 10 000 kilometres of coast. This is more than half the coastal length of the United States of America. The comparison with other countries becomes more marked when population size is considered. For every million Americans, there are 94 kilometres of coast, compared with 3333 kilometres for every million New Zealanders.

The coastal dimension is one of the country's greatest assets. Few New Zealanders grow up without ready access to a beach where they can swim, fish, clamber over rocks or take a boat onto the water. The beautiful and uncrowded coastline is so much a part of life in New Zealand that it is usually taken for granted.

There are good practical reasons for living close to the sea as Maori and pakeha have mostly chosen to do. The earliest settlements were sited on the coast to be near its food resources—the fish that swim in the ocean and those that stay in their shells close to the shore. The sea offered a highway for transporting people and things, so good harbours were the preferred sites for settlement. There is, however, a stronger pull that draws man to the meeting place of land and sea. Perhaps it is linked with the origins of life, an unconscious bond that attracts human beings back to the watery confines from which life first emerged to establish itself on land. Whatever the elemental attachment, to observe the powerful surf rolling onto an empty sweep of sand or breaking against a rocky headland is to inspire the imagination and to feed the human spirit.

The form of this book, an aerial circumnavigation of the North and South Islands, enables us to discover the infinite variations along the merging line of land and sea and to appreciate anew New Zealand's magnificent coastal scenery. We are able to include most of the main features of New Zealand as a whole; because of the country's long and narrow shape, there is no sharp division between coast and interior. A few areas outside the coastal zone have had to be excluded but in general this visual record presents a comprehensive picture of New Zealand. It reflects the main landforms, land uses and distinctive regional characteristics. The coast contains the main population centres as well as the remotest corners of the country.

This project—systematically flying around the coast to photograph it for a book and television series—has produced a unique overview of New Zealand. Only a fraction of what has been recorded is reproduced, but the main impressions from the experience are reflected here.

Undoubtedly the most striking impression is the incredible diversity of scenery. The contrasts exist not only between north and south but also within relatively short distances. The climate and topography of the coastline are constantly changing. Along a 100-kilometre stretch of the South Island's West Coast, for instance, we pass dense rainforest, barren plateaux, lush dairying plains, forbidding bluffs and rolling sheep country. New Zealand's overseas tourist promotion capitalises on the country's variety. One advertisement shows a composite map of Alaska, England, Norway, Switzerland and Japan and lists New Zealand's attractions: beaches that rival Hawaii's, beautiful fiords like those of Norway, majestic Alps like Switzerland's and so on. It is arguable whether each feature is greater or lesser than another country's. Beauty is in the eye of the beholder, and New Zealanders tend to be more subjective and defensive about the beauty of their country than are most people. However, it would be difficult to find in such a small territory anywhere else a landscape that encompasses such variety.

Another powerful impression is the country's youth in terms of its geology and its human history. There are signs of active mountain building, from the Southern Alps to the volcanic landscapes of the north. The unstable nature of the land is emphasised by the dramatic erosion that scars the countryside, especially where native vegetation has been cleared.

This country has not mellowed over centuries of close liaison between man and nature. In the brief period since European colonisation began, the two have commonly been in conflict. There is a harshness resulting from the single minded effort to conquer the land. Instead of complementing the surroundings as they do in older societies, human surroundings often have a jarring temporary look about them. The late entry of New Zealand into the inhabited realms of the world has at least enabled much of its natural beauty to be preserved. Its three million people have an enviable amount of glorious unspoiled land, surrounded by clear unpolluted air and water.

In the last century, New Zealanders have become an urbanised people. Although the economy is still firmly based on the land, the proportion of the population living in towns and cities has doubled to 80 per cent. For the city dweller, this book is a reminder how small a part of the country is closely populated. In an overcrowded world, the New Zealander is indeed fortunate to have access to so much open space.

The lofty perspective of our aerial vantage point opens up an appreciation of New Zealand denied the earthbound onlooker. Overall patterns are instantly revealed in a detached but exhilarating vision. Human endeavour seems a small and puny scratching on the grand design and details that appear ugly and chaotic from the ground acquire orderliness and beauty when viewed from the air. The softening of ugliness is one effect, but more valuable is the way the map comes to life. A single hill that dominates the ground-based view becomes part of a range; rivers and sea, hills and harbours seen in isolation are transformed into a greater whole.

On a lower level, the aerial view can satisfy our curiosity as it reveals backyards and swimming pools or the whole context of familiar buildings and landmarks that normally display only one facade. The still photograph cannot completely capture the soaring freedom from the force of gravity or the omnipotent feeling gained in flight, but it can freeze the moments of exhilaration and allow us to contemplate the patterns of nature and mankind within which we live.

HALF TITLE PAGE A typical pastoral scene. These sheep are grazing in the Tank Paddocks, Geraldine Downs, near Canterbury. In the background is the Four Peaks Range.

TITLE PAGE Looking across the Firth of Thames towards Auckland from Waikawau, Coromandel Peninsula. It is twilight and a storm broods over in the west.

FOREWORD Sheep graze on the green hills near Lawrence, Otago.

CONTENTS PAGE Grey peaks in the Mount Isobel Ranges, seen from Conical Hill, Hanmer Springs, North Canterbury. A forestry plantation in the foreground submits to a passing shower.

Cape Reinga
North Cape
Parengarenga Harbour
Ninety   Aupori Peninsula
Mile   Doubtless Bay
Beach   Whangaroa Harbour
                   Cavalli Islands
Ahipara Bay   Bay of Islands
        Kaitaia   Kerikeri   Cape Brett
            Taipa   Waitangi
                   Paihia   Russell
            Rawene   Whangaruru Harbour
        Opononi   Kaikohe
Hokianga Harbour
        Waipoua   Tutukaka
                   Whangarei
                   Bream Head
Dargaville

                Maungaturoto
                                Little Barrier
                                Island
North Head   Great Barrier Island
Kaipara Harbour   Wellsford
South Head   Kawau Island
                Orewa
                Hauraki Gulf
        Takapuna   Coromandel   Whitianga
Piha   AUCKLAND
        Firth of
Manukau Harbour   Thames
                Thames
                        Whangamata
Port Waikato
                        Matakana Island   Cape Runaway
            Huntly   Tauranga Harbour   Hicks Bay
        Ngaruawahia   Mayor Island
                Hamilton   Mt Maunganui   White Island   East
Raglan Harbour   Tauranga   Rangitaiki Motu   Tukitiki   Cape
                            Te Puke   River   River   Ruatoria
                Kaimai Range   Raukumara   Te Puia
Kawhia Harbour   Matata   Whakatane   Range
            Kawhia   Kawerau Opotiki   Tokomaru Bay
                    Rotorua   Mt Tarawera
                                Kawhenue   Tolaga Bay
            Te Kuiti   Range
                                            Ormond   Gable End
Awakino   Te Taupo   Gisborne   Foreland
Mokau River   Poverty Bay
Tongaporutu   Young Nicks Head
North Taranaki Bight
            Waitara   Wairoa Wairoa River
        New Plymouth   Mohaka Mohaka River
            Inglewood   Viaduct   Mahia Peninsula
Cape Egmont   Mt Egmont
            Stratford
        Opunake   Eltham   Napier
            Manaia   Aropaoanui
                Hawera   Tukituki River
South Taranaki Bight   Patea   Hastings   Cape Kidnappers
                    Wanganui   Waimarama
            Wanganui River
                    Ratana
                    Feilding
                Rangitikei River   Porangahau
Farewell Spit   Palmerston North
                Manawatu River   Cape Turnagain
Golden Bay   Levin
            Stephens Island   Tararua
                        Otaki   Ranges
Heaphy River Totaranui   D'Urville   Waikanae   Castlepoint
            Tasman Bay Island Kapiti   Masterton
        Karamea   French Pass   Upper Hutt
            Motueka   Pelorus   Lake Wairarapa
                Sound WELLINGTON Rimutaka
            Nelson Queen Charlotte   Lower Hutt Range
                Sound   Palliser
                Picton   Bay
                    Blenheim   Cape Palliser
Cape Foulwind   Seddon
        Westport Denniston
Charleston   Inland
            Paparoa   Kaikoura   Cape Campbell
Punakaiki   Range   Range
                    Seaward
Greymouth   Kaikoura
            Kumara   Clarence River
Arahura River   Hanmer   Kaikoura
Hokitika   Springs
            Culverden   Cheviot
Wanganui Bluff
        Okarito   Motunau
Waiho River   Franz Josef   Pegasus Bay
        Glacier
            Southern Alps   Kaiapoi
Bruce Bay   Fox Glacier   Waimakariri River
Lake Moeraki
        Haast   Mt Cook   CHRISTCHURCH
            Lake   Lake
Jackson Bay   Tekapo   Ellesmere   Akaroa
Cascade Point   Rakaia River   Banks Peninsula
                Ashburton
            Lake   Ashburton River
Martins Bay   Wanaka   Geraldine
                Rangitata River
Milford Sound
            Lake   Timaru
Bligh Sound Wanaka
George Sound   Wainomo Lagoon
            Waitaki River
Charles Sound   Waitaki River
        Murchison   Oamaru
ful Sound   Mountains Lake
        Te Anau Alexandra
    Kepler Te Anau   Moeraki
    Mountains
ksea Sound   Manapouri   Karitane
on Island   Manapouri
Sound   Otago Peninsula
        Riversdale   Lawrence   DUNEDIN
vation Inlet
gur Point   Gore   Balclutha
Long Point   Te Waewae   Clutha River
        Bay   Catlins River
    INVERCARGILL
        Fortrose
Bluff   Toetoes Bay   Curio Bay
    Foveaux Strait
    Oban
        Muttonbird Islands
        Stewart Island

West Coast

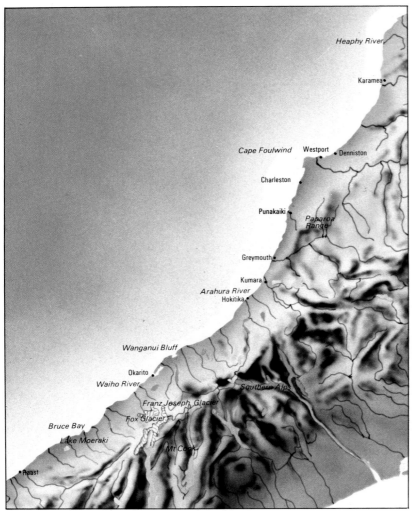

The first European sighting of New Zealand was recorded by Abel Tasman when he wrote in his log on 13 December 1642, 'We saw a great land uplifted high'. From the sea that bears his name, the Dutch explorer was observing the Alpine ridge that rises from the narrow coastal strip on the west coast of the South Island and extends along most of its length.

Here, like Tasman, we begin our discovery of the splendidly varied New Zealand coastline. Of all the regions we will be flying over, this and the adjoining Fiordland have been least disturbed by the hand of man. The area retains the primeval quality of a country hundreds of millions of years in the making. The first people arrived from East Polynesia a mere thousand years ago. Its pristine beauty can be savoured in the dense rainforests, alive with birdsong, or in the awesome emptiness of the silent mountains. Each end of the West Coast contains the country's oldest rocks, formed 600 million years ago and forced apart by the upward thrusting mountain block of the Southern Alps during the last five million years.

The Alps dictate the Coast's climate, piercing the clouds that blow in from the Tasman Sea and precipitating large amounts of rain on their western side. The Alps also form a barrier that isolates the region from the rest of the country and nurtures a distinctive personality — 'the Coaster'. There are not many of them, considering the size of the region (80 per cent of it is uninhabited) but their independent hospitable character has made an indelible contribution to New Zealand's folklore.

Gold lured the first Europeans here in the 1860s. Within two or three years the population exploded to about the same size it is today. After gold, the Coast's other assets (coal, timber, and land) were exploited; the recent history of the area, however, has been one of economic decline except in tourism.

Our course along the West Coast is plotted in the opposite direction to that of Abel Tasman, starting in the north and progressing towards Fiordland. In the north-west corner there is a range of mountains named after Tasman; it was at this point that he departed from the South Island after a violent confrontation with the Maoris. From the air we can follow the forest-clad ridges to where they meet the Tasman Sea in a series of precipitous cliffs and headlands. The only other way to observe this territory is on foot and the best known section for trampers is the track that follows part of the Heaphy River. A road had been proposed here to link the West Coast with Nelson's Golden Bay but the idea caused a public outcry against the destruction of virgin forest and bush. As a result, the road still stops near Karamea, the most northerly settlement on the Coast. Its pocket of flat fertile dairying land comes as a relief among the rugged ranges that plummet to the water's edge along the north-west coast. Karamea, with the rest of the area to beyond Westport, is part of Buller, a district that has been included in Nelson Province for administrative purposes.

The northward approach to Westport shows the first signs of Buller's source of wealth — coal. High on a desolate plateau is Stockton open cast mine; its exposed seams of shiny black coal are linked to the railhead below at Ngakawau by eight kilometres of cableway. The bituminous product, found only in Buller, is New Zealand's highest grade coal. It is extracted underground at other mines, some marked by the forlorn remnants of once thriving communities.

The mountains retreat from the coast at Westport and low lying land extends southwest from the town out to Cape Foulwind. Much of this land is soggy *pakihi* (barren soil) of little use for farming. Limestone at the Cape is used with local coal in the country's largest cement works; the tall chimneys dominate an otherwise empty skyline. Further south the coastline presents more varied and attractive scenery with the best known feature being halfway between Westport and Greymouth, at Punakaiki. An eroded formation of layered limestone, it is known as the Pancake Rocks because it looks like stacks of giant pancakes. Through blowholes, the sea blasts spectacular showers of spray.

Mostly it is a wild and rugged coast, tamed at the mouths of rivers like the Buller and the Grey, the setting for the towns of Westport and Greymouth and the only two ports on the Coast. Greymouth is the main commercial centre handling coal, timber and, to a lesser extent, agricultural products. The third town, Hokitika, is 40 kilometres south of Greymouth and half its size with a population of 3500, but soon after it sprouted into existence it was described as 'the most rising place on earth'.

The romance of the West Coast is largely the legacy of those few heady years after the gold rush started in 1864. Miners from the declining fields of Otago and Australia poured in and threw up their shanty settlements all along the coast. They feverishly panned the rivers, harvesting the pick of the alluvial deposits within a few years. Then it became necessary to construct water races for sluicing, and finally massive dredges were used to extract the gold specks economically.

Maoris had little use for gold but their most precious material came from the same area. It was nephrite, also known as greenstone or jade, which is washed down the Arahura and Taramakau Rivers. From here it was taken throughout pre European New Zealand to be painstakingly crafted into weapons, tools and exquisite ornaments.

South from Hokitika there are only a few scattered population pockets; there is very little farm land cleared from the bush and the natural vegetation and landforms are little disturbed by human activity. It is a fresh green forested country, overshadowed by the eternally snow-capped peaks of the Southern Alps. Numerous rivers roll down from the mountains to join the thundering Tasman Sea.

Towards the end of this section of our journey is the Westland National Park which stretches from the coast to the tops of the soaring mountains. The jewels in its glistening crown are undoubtedly the twin glaciers, Fox and Franz Josef.

Not all visitors have expressed unreserved admiration for the West Coast. Captain Cook called it 'an inhospitable shore, unworthy of observation except for its ridge of naked and barren rocks covered with snow'. But today, when its unspoiled qualities are much rarer, few would agree.

A GREAT LAND **When Abel Tasman first saw the South Island's Alpine Range, he described it as 'a great land uplifted high'.**

HEAPHY RIVER **The sea is discoloured by vegetation from the magnificent bush flanking the famous Heaphy Track which links the West Coast and Golden Bay. The river runs through the Northwest Nelson Forest Park from the mountains to the Tasman Sea.**

DAIRY COUNTRY NEAR KARAMEA **A rich pocket of flat farmland contrasts with the wild cliffs that mark most of the north-west coastline. Behind the plains are the rugged mountains of the Matiri Range. Mild temperatures from warm sea currents and a good rainfall make it an ideal area for dairying. This part of the coast is also a potential source of oil and gas.**

SLIPPING CLIFFS, LITTLE WANGANUI **These sandstone bluffs subsiding into the sea are a reminder of how the land is constantly changing. The cliffs are comparatively young — ten million years.**

ROCKY SHORE **The Grenadier Rocks are dwarfed by a steep headland in this view north towards Karamea from the mouth of the Waimarie River. In contrast with its exposed, rugged coastline, the region maintains a lush greenness all year round. The road winds between the steep hills and the sea, passing through areas of flax, nikau and cabbage trees.**

BARREN LOWLANDS **The mountains begin to recede from the coast north of Westport between Birchfield and Granity but the flat land is of little use. It is leached and waterlogged pakihi.**

14

COAL SEAM, STOCKTON **Open cast mining has revealed a layer of bituminous coal which in parts is 12 metres thick. New Zealand's best quality coal, it is sent by cableway to the railhead at Ngakawau. South of Stockton is an underground mine which has been burning since 1926.**

DERELICT DENNISTON INCLINE **The Incline was built in 1880 to deliver coal to the railway below. At the time it was considered a great engineering feat, but it has been superseded by trucks since a road was put in. Nevertheless, 30 million tonnes of coal left the West Coast via the Incline.**

WESTPORT DOCKS **The port was originally built for the major export of coal but today the ships are more likely to be handling cement or fish. The tuna industry is developing as a result of pressure on overseas fisheries resources.**

DESERTED **Remnants of the old gold mining town of Charleston in an otherwise empty view towards Westport. With the gold gone, the raised beach has been reclaimed by scrub. Even during the boom years, the rugged coastline made it difficult for ships to bring food in for the gold seekers.**

Gatefold over: SWEEP OF BEACH **This unnamed beach just south of Bruce Bay is typical of several on the south Westland coast, which contains magnificent virgin scenery where the mountains begin to crowd in on the sea and the forest reaches down to the edge of deserted beaches.**

COAL BEARING HILLS **The southern end of the Paparoa Range looms over a typically grey sea The names of the bluffs — Twelve Mile Bluff, Fourteen Mile Bluff — describe their distance north of Greymouth. In the valleys a short distance inland there are a number of coalmines.**

PANCAKE ROCKS **This weird formation at Punakaiki between Westport and Greymouth has been created by the eroding action of the sea on the stratified limestone rock. It is a well known stopping point for travellers, who may be treated to a spectacular display of water spouting through the blowholes.**

TIROMOANA **The road between Greymouth and Westport hugs the rocky coastal edge of the rich coal bearing Paparoa Range. In the far distance is Cape Foulwind, named by Captain Cook when he encountered adverse weather conditions there.**

Gatefold left: MOUNT TASMAN **At 3497 metres, this is the second highest peak in New Zealand. Only Mount Cook is higher. The route to the summit has attracted climbers for almost eighty years.**

GREIGS SETTLEMENT **A scattering of holiday cottages or baches on the wild coast north of Greymouth. The houses have been placed to take advantage of the nearby beach with its opportunities for fishing and swimming. The surrounding bush offers interesting walks and plenty of firewood.**

GOLD TAILINGS, TARAMAKAU RIVER **In 1876 there were over 4000 miners panning for gold here. Later, sluicing and dredging methods were used, leaving behind huge mounds of river shingle or tailings. Their pinkish colour is caused by a type of fungus growth.**

HOKITIKA **In its heyday, this town was New Zealand's third most important port because of the gold found in the area. It now serves the surrounding farms and forests. The solid grey church in the right foreground is evidence of the large population of Irish Catholics who flocked to the goldfields over a century ago.**

LOGGING, IANTHE FOREST **Timber was a resource to be exploited, but recent conservation pressure has led to a policy of selection logging to preserve native forests. This star felling pattern should remove less than a quarter of the rimu trees.**

GREENSTONE SOURCE, ARAHURA VALLEY **Maoris crossed the Southern Alps for the specific purpose of collecting the nephrite or greenstone that lay in this tortuous valley not far from Hokitika. The tough and beautiful stone was made into fine cutting tools, as well as weapons and ornaments.**

GREENSTONE MANUFACTURE, HOKITIKA **Machine technology continues the Maori tradition of making greenstone jewellery. After being lifted out of the mountains by helicopter, the boulders are cut with diamond saws and then shaped mainly into tourist souvenirs.**

FRANZ JOSEF GLACIER This and the Fox Glacier are the star attractions of the Westland National Park. They are unique for a temperate country such as New Zealand because they reach so close to sea level. The Franz Josef Glacier, 12 kilometres long, has had its movement measured at the rate of a metre and a half a day. At the bottom of the valley scoured out by the glacier, melting ice forms into the Waiho River.

OKARITO LAGOON The south end in the distance was the site of a booming gold town. At the north end of the lagoon is the only nesting place in New Zealand for the beautiful white heron.

CREVASSES, FRANZ JOSEF GLACIER **The fractures on the surface of the glacier are the result of stress caused by the uneven movement of the 'river of ice'. The sides of the 'river' move more slowly than the middle because of the friction against the schist walls. Crevasses do not extend to the moving mass of ice beneath.**

Over: FRANZ JOSEF NÉVÉ **The northern section of the mountain walls that rise almost perpendicularly from the edge of the snowfields that feed the glacier. The annual snowfall at this altitude is over 60 metres.**

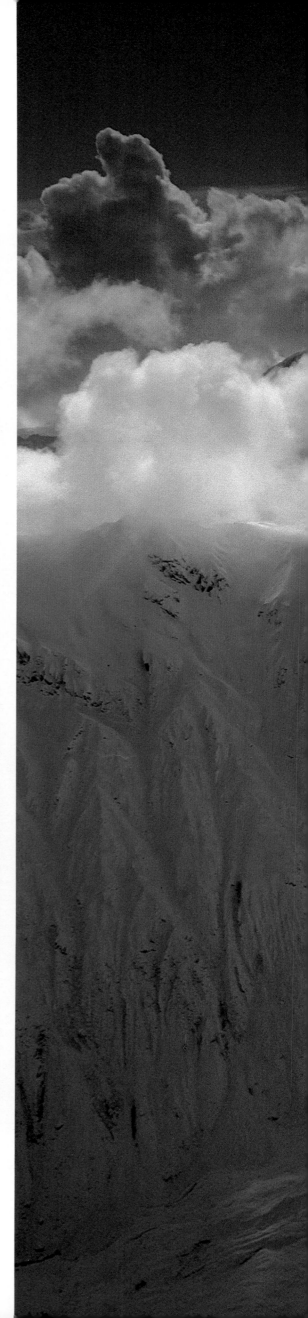

SMOKING WATER One of the many waterfalls into the Waiho River on its path from the terminal of the Franz Josef Glacier to the Tasman Sea. The river rises beneath the glacier and, when its icy water comes into contact with warm air, it produces a thin layer of fog. This is why it is called 'waiho'—smoking water. Because of the area's high rainfall, the river is often in flood.

Right: FOX GLACIER SNOWFIELD Sculpted snow and ice at the head of the Fox Glacier, the largest and grandest on the western side of the Southern Alps. The soft snow becomes packed down into hard ice and, as the pressure builds, the ice begins to slide down the mountain valley as a glacier.

HIGHLAND FLOWERS **The beautiful** *Clematis paniculata* **flowers on a climbing plant entwined around branches high in Westland's beech forests.**

NEW PLANT LIFE **The Fox and Franz Josef Glaciers are presently in a stage of retreat. The first sign of plant regeneration is the appearance of mosses and lichens on the exposed rocks. The decomposing lichens provide a base for larger plants.**

Over: KARANGARUA RIVER MOUTH **Looking south over the entrance to the Karangarua River. To the left is Hunt beach. On the first headland is Makawhio Point and behind the second headland is Bruce Bay.**

FISHING RETREAT, MORAKI The fisherman can choose between surfcasting on the beach and angling for trout on one of the lakes that are scattered among the bush-covered hills of south Westland. Apart from fishing lodges, there are few permanent habitations in this peaceful setting.

AWESOME ALPS The jagged ridges and vertical faces of the Southern Alps viewed from above the Haast Valley. The massive mountain range rises steeply from the narrow plains of the West Coast reaching the highest point—3763 metres—on Mount Cook's summit. It presents a formidable challenge to mountaineers.

Left: HAAST RIVER Clear mountain water pours down the 27-metre drop of Thundercreek Falls into the canyon carved out by the river. The Falls are reached by a short track from the Haast Road through silver beech forest.

Far left: BRUCE BAY The rimu forest reaches to the edge of the sea in one of the South Westland State Forests where the timber industry and conservationists have been in dispute.

Fiordland

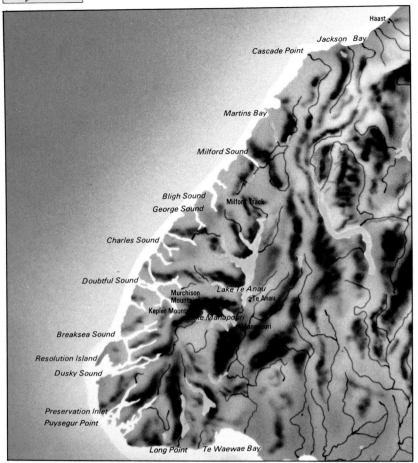

It would be hard to find anywhere a more impressive area of natural beauty and grandeur than Fiordland. It is an uncompromising beauty that invites great admiration but that forbids too close a contact. People are intruders here and are kept at arm's length as observers of some of Nature's excesses. The whole southwest corner has been sealed off as a National Park because it is a unique wilderness worthy of preservation and also because it is hostile to settlement and exploitation.

Fiordland National Park is larger than all the others put together. It consists of a jumbled mass of steep mountains and impenetrable forests between magnificent lakes that mark the eastern boundary and a coastline indented by deep fiords. Both the lakes and the fiords have been gouged out of the resistant rock by ancient glaciers. In places the mountain walls rise almost vertically from the water and at their highest, near Milford Sound, reach over 2500 metres. The peaks are usually hidden by cloud; Fiordland has a very heavy rainfall, and is one of the wettest places in the world. Its mountain sides are frequently veiled in cascades of water—part of the beauty which both attracts and repels visitors. For much of the year the only humans in the area are the fishermen working in the very deep waters offshore.

This most deserted region of New Zealand once harboured most of its European population. After Captain Cook spent a month in Dusky Sound in 1773, sealers followed and a party marooned there in 1792 formed the first pakeha settlement. But since the sealing and whaling days ended, Fiordland has largely resisted human encroachment. Some areas are still unexplored.

For most people, Westland's southern border is at the Haast River where the main road turns inland towards Otago, but there is a coastal road that continues south for another 50 kilometres past the Arawata rivermouth, petering out at Jackson Bay. The hope of finding gold here attracted prospectors such as the legendary Arawata Bill, immortalised in Denis Glover's poems.

The riches of the sea are all that bring men now to the little harbour below the sheltering hills of Jackson Head. In the 1870s there were grandiose ideas for a special settlement at Jackson Bay to which European immigrants were sent, but its isolation was never overcome and the scheme failed.

Between Jackson and Martins Bays, the transition from Westland to Fiordland becomes apparent at Cascade Point. From this bleak headland the southern coast is 'everlasting forest and hill' as the pioneer hydrological surveyors of the *Acheron* observed in 1850. The topography becomes progressively steeper and more rugged, culminating in the mighty Darran Mountains that stand sentinel over the northernmost and grandest of the fiords—Milford Sound.

Probably the most often photographed New Zealand scenic view is that of Mitre Peak's steep sides mirrored in the deep blue water of Milford Sound. It is certainly the most spectacular fiord, but others that are longer and as beautiful are rarely visited. Milford alone can be easily reached by road or on foot. The approach by car or bus passes magnificent mountain scenery and terminates at the head of the Sound where there is a first-class hotel. The famous walk begins at the northern end of Lake Te Anau and takes three or four days with overnight stops in huts along the way. The first section through the Clinton Valley follows the forested riverbank and on the frequent days of torrential rain the valley walls come alive with cascading water. Then the track zigzags over the Mackinnon Pass, which provides breathtaking views of the ice-scoured canyon and in the other direction towards Milford. In the last stage there is a side track to the Sutherland Falls, long thought to be the highest in the world, and the walk ends at the appropriately named Sandfly Point.

From Milford Sound our coastal progression takes us south past a number of lesser-known fiords—Bligh, George, Caswell, Charles, Nancy and Thompson Sounds. Then we reach one of the longest and perhaps most beautiful Sounds—Doubtful Sound. Its name originated in Captain Cook's reluctance to enter the Sound as he feared that there would be insufficient wind to sail the *Endeavour* out again. However, the depth of the water was more than adequate. Sheer rock walls plunge hundreds of metres below the sea along Doubtful Sound's 160-kilometre coastline. It is shared by seals, penguins, dolphins and the occasional launch probing its countless bays and islets. The public has recently gained access to the Sound over a road between Lake Manapouri and Deep Cove, built in conjunction with the country's largest hydro-electric power scheme.

The proposal to raise the level of Lake Manapouri as part of the project caused a torrent of protest, which was a turning point for the growing conservation movement in the 1960s. It produced the largest petition ever presented to Parliament and contributed to the downfall of the National government in 1972. The scheme eventually went ahead without any alteration in the lake level.

Manapouri is fed by Lake Te Anau, the largest South Island lake, which is 66 kilometres long with three fiords branching west into wild mountainous terrain. The Murchison Mountains between the South and Middle Fiords have restricted entry to protect the takahe, one of the world's rarest birds. Flightless and about the size of a hen, they were thought to be extinct until 1948 when Dr Geoffrey Orbell discovered them in what is now known as Takahe Valley. Another very rare bird, the kakapo, is confined mainly to the Milford Sound area.

The eastern side of the narrow lake is much flatter and drier than the rainforest shoreline on the west. Here on the open moraine lies Te Anau township, where most visitors enter Fiordland National Park. One road out leads to Manapouri; another follows the lake north to Milford Sound.

Returning to the southwest coast, we reach an area significant in New Zealand's earliest European history. The southern fiords were the first landfall for sailing ships following the path of the 'Roaring Forties'. Captain Cook's *Resolution* arrived here in 1773 and stayed in Dusky Sound for several weeks.

Others who followed were more interested in the seal colonies than the beauties of nature. In 1792 a gang of sealers was left at Dusky, the first shipwreck occurred and pakeha settlement was under way. Sealers and whalers had gone by the middle of the nineteenth century and the next disturbance was the discovery of gold at Preservation Inlet. Since then the most impregnable part of New Zealand has kept its secrets to itself, retaining its timeless beauty for future onlookers.

REMOTE AND FORBIDDING **The Fiordland coast is a serrated edge of steep mountains and ravines, penetrated by the sea. This is Doubtful Sound.**

CASCADE POINT **On the horizon between Fiordland and Westland, this rocky tongue of land looms over a sea that is 1800 metres deep. The last populated section recedes on the northern horizon.**

WHITEBAITING, OKURU RIVER **The West Coast river mouths provide most of the whitebait catch. The young fish are netted during their migration from salt water to fresh water.**

Left: END OF THE ROAD **Jackson Bay, the southern terminus of the West Coast road, is a haven for commercial fishermen. It had pretensions towards being a grander settlement when founded in 1875.**

Right: HAAST TOWNSHIP **This little timber town began as a construction camp for the completion of the Haast Pass road. The bridge (top right) is part of the link between Otago and the West Coast.**

RUBY BEACH **This area between Martins Bay and Milford Sound sees the occasional fisherman in search of crayfish or rock lobsters. There are also several seal colonies along the coast.**

BOWEN FALLS, MILFORD **The water roars down a 160-metre drop into the sea. These falls leap in two steps from a high glacial hanging valley, and their energy is used to generate electric power for the nearby hotel. Tourist launches moored at the wharf are dwarfed by the sheer mountain walls.**

Left: HOLLYFORD RIVER MOUTH **Lake McKerrow (top) was probably the northernmost fiord before the land was raised and the Hollyford River had to negotiate a sand bar to reach the ocean.**

MACKINNON PASS The highest point of the famous Milford Track, which is open only in summer, when it is normally clear of snow.

MILFORD TRACK Looking over the Mackinnon Pass back to Clinton Canyon, where what is known as 'the finest walk in the world' follows a river shaded by magnificent forest. The 54-kilometre-long Milford Track was open only to guided parties for many years, but now it is available to others.

LAKE QUILL This lake is the reservoir for one of the highest waterfalls in the world, the Sutherland Falls (long thought to be the highest waterfall in the world). From the narrow spout (left) the water drops almost 600 metres. Lake Quill was named after the daring surveyor who climbed up the fall.

GEORGE SOUND This is one of thirteen fiords along the inhospitable southwest coast. Glaciers have carved steep-sided troughs which were invaded by the sea at the end of the last ice age 15 000 years ago.

MILFORD SOUND A view looking towards the head of the most spectacular fiord of all. Named for the southern Welsh town of Milford Haven, it was first visited by Maoris in search of greenstone. The walls rising vertically to a height of 1200 metres from the sea are the highest sea cliffs in the world.

CHARLES SOUND ENTRANCE One of the most remote fiords of all, Charles Sound is about halfway along the Fiordland coast. In this part of Fiordland, the New Zealand shelf is extremely narrow, almost non-existent in places, and there are strong currents in the very deep water.

DOUBTFUL SOUND **A break in the ever-present cloud cover reveals part of the long, narrow Sound. It received its name because Captain Cook was doubtful of getting a wind to take him out in reasonable time.**

Over: SOUTHERN ALPS FROM ABOVE TE ANAU **A splendid chaos of mountains, resembling an ocean petrified during a storm. Mount Cook stands out boldly on the horizon (centre).**

LAKE MANAPOURI **From above the Kepler Range, north of the lake, this dark expanse of water hides the beauty once threatened by a hydro power scheme.**

TAKAHE VALLEY **In 1948 the takahe, a flightless bird thought to be extinct, was rediscovered in the snow tussock grassland of the Murchison mountains.**

MURCHISON MOUNTAINS **Looking down on Lake Te Anau, the eastern border of Fiordland, from above the mountains that are closed to the public so that the rare takahe may be protected.**

Right: TE ANAU TOWNSHIP **This tourist gateway to the Fiordland National Park is perched on a moraine plain, facing the rugged country on the other side of the South Island's largest lake.**

MANAPOURI VILLAGE AND LAKE One of the loveliest lakes in New Zealand, tranquil and unspoiled, it is dotted with wooded islands and encircled by gentle beaches beneath bush covered slopes. The village near the outlet at the eastern end of the lake caters to the tourist.

CASCADE COVE, DUSKY SOUND This is a narrow inlet in New Zealand's largest fiord. On his second voyage in 1773, Captain Cook brought the *Resolution* into Dusky Sound to refresh his men and to repair the ship. Dusky Sound remains unchanged since Cook's day.

Right: WEST ARM, MANAPOURI At the head of this arm is the Manapouri hydro-electric power station, with underground turbines and a tunnel that discharges the water through the Main Divide and into Doubtful Sound.

BREAKSEA ISLAND **The steep and bush-covered island in the foreground stands guard in the middle of the entrance to lonely Breaksea Sound. Cook wrote in 1773 that he had called the island Breaksea Isle 'because it effectually covers this entrance from the violence of the SW swell'.**

PRESERVATION INLET **This southernmost fiord is usually visited only by fishermen. In earlier days, it offered a welcome refuge for sealers and whalers from the stormy seas of Foveaux Strait. Its isolation was briefly interrupted at the end of the last century, when some gold was discovered there.**

COASTAL WALK, SOUTH FIORDLAND **A swing bridge near a hut in the centre of the picture indicates an isolated walking track that crosses the Wairaurahiri River on the south coast.**

Left: WESTERN FOVEAUX STRAIT **Once past Puysegur Point on the southwest corner of the South Island, mountains and fiords give way to a flatter and windswept coastal landscape.**

Right: SEAL ISLANDS, DUSKY SOUND **These islands appear to float on the surface of the water near the historic area where Captain Cook spent a month in 1773. It has remained almost untouched.**

Southland, Otago

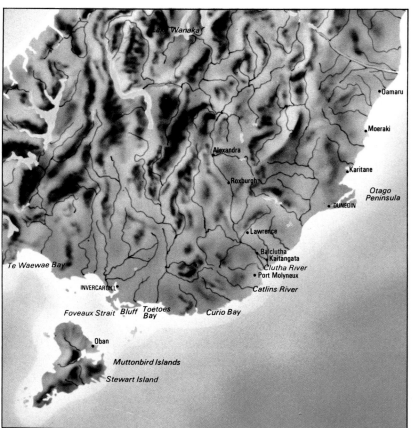

With some justification, this region can been called the Scotland of the South. This is not just because of the Gaelic placenames, the burr in the regional dialect or the sturdy build of its fair-skinned inhabitants. The link with Scotland is also there in the landscape, veiled by grey mists in the same way as the Scottish countryside. The rich, evergreen pastures lining most of the southeast coast testify to the Scottish tradition of careful husbandry and the Calvinist dedication to hard work. They produce a higher yield of meat and wool than anywhere else in the country, in spite of a harsh climate that gives the shortest grass-growing season.

However, at least eight centuries before the Presbyterian settlement of Otago and Southland began, moa hunters lived on this coast, pursuing the huge flightless birds to their extinction. The Maoris who remained were the southernmost Polynesians, far removed in distance and environment from their tropical homelands. Unable to cultivate the kumara or sweet potato, they were hunters and gatherers, relying for food on the plentiful animals, birds and fish of the coastal region. Later the seals and whales attracted the first European adventurers, who established a vigorous trade in the early nineteenth century from a string of stations along the wild southern extremity.

Traces of the untamed land can still be seen in the Catlins area of the southeast, but the plains on either side have a thoroughly settled permanency, remarkably consolidated after only 130 years.

After leaving the stormy and deserted southwest corner of Fiordland, the mountains start receding by the time we enter the large sweep of Te Waewae Bay. Here is the first of the alluvial plains that support Southland's farming wealth and here also are the first signs that we are back in civilisation. The roading system resumes again and settlements appear near the mouth of the Waiau River.

Around the next rocky point are some attractive holiday beaches, including Riverton, which claims to be the oldest settlement in the province. Its roots go back to the boisterous whaling days. Whalers were the earliest settlers to appreciate the agricultural potential of the southern plains when they turned their attention inland from the sea. That potential was lost on the surveyor who was preparing the way in the 1840s for planned emigration from Scotland. He rejected the area around Invercargill for settlement, describing it as 'a mere bog, unfit for human habitation'. Some patches of the swamp that discouraged him still exist, but most of the area has been converted into productive farmland.

The appearance of the rolling pastures softened in the glow of Southland's long twilights can be deceptive. The land is not naturally fertile. Large-scale drainage and fertilisation have been necessary to correct the soil deficiencies and the leaching caused by the high rainfall of the area. However, all the rain keeps the paddocks green throughout the year and frees the Southland farmer from the fear of drought that plagues his counterparts in the rest of the country.

Invercargill is heavily dependent on the farmer, but it does have some secondary industry. However, the distance from markets handicaps manufacturers and the lack of sunshine discourages workers from living there. The city has benefited from the aluminium

smelter built at Tiwai Point by an overseas consortium when they were offered cheap hydro-electric power. The smelter is sited here because it is close to the power source at Lake Manapouri and to Southland's port at Bluff, where ships can unload the bauxite from Australia. Bluff is a modern containerised port equipped to export the province's primary produce, but it is best known as the base for the fishing fleet that harvests Bluff oysters.

Following the trail of the oyster boats across Foveaux Strait takes us to New Zealand's third main island. Its climate is warmer than Southland's, the gold sand beaches are fringed with virgin bush and there are virtually no roads, only tracks for exploring the island's beauty on foot. The tiny populated area is on the lip of Paterson Inlet, which cuts halfway across the island from the east.

The southeast corner of the South Island is another wilderness area with a treacherous coastline that has seen many shipwrecks. The worst was in 1881 when 131 people were drowned after the *Tararua* hit a reef off Waipipi Point. Between the rocky headlands and steep cliffs is a series of stunning curved beaches, dissected by numerous rivers and streams and backed by rain-soaked forest. This is the little known edge of the Catlins State Forest Park, from which large amounts of timber were extracted last century. The remaining stands of trees are mostly reserved and the old settlements have been left to the birds. The coast here has a rich marine life, including colonies of penguins and seals.

Forest makes way for farms as we move along the South Otago coast towards the mouth of the Clutha River. Its smooth plains are very fertile, particularly on the island of Inchclutha, but the riches that the river has given, it has also taken away in mighty floods.

The Clutha carries a much greater volume of water than any other New Zealand river. Its potential for hydro-electric power has been tapped at Roxburgh, but a much larger scheme is planned nearer its source. The Clutha starts in the three magnificent lakes of Wanaka, Hawea and Wakatipu. The bare land it traverses in Central Otago contrasts sharply with the green coastal region.

On a tributary of the Clutha River at Lawrence where the two distinct Otago regions merge, began the Otago gold rush in 1861, thirteen years after the arrival of the first Presbyterian settlers in their 'New Edinburgh'. After the find at Lawrence became known, the *Otago Witness* reported: 'Last Sunday the congregation at Church consisted of the minister and the precentor.' Hordes of newcomers joined the gold seekers and new fields inland were opened. Dunedin became the largest city in the colony and began showing its prosperity in bricks and stone. Many of the solid, ornately ornamented buildings have survived to give Dunedin its special character, an air of permanence and civilisation. One of the finest examples of its Victorian architecture is Otago University, New Zealand's first and a key ingredient in the flavour of the city.

North of Dunedin is one of the loveliest stretches of coast in the country. The gentle hills of North Otago roll down to meet the ocean amidst rocky outcrops or on smooth sand beaches such as Warrington, Waikouaiti, Karitane and Moeraki. The shoreline becomes even after Oamaru, an attractive town with architectural distinction created by the use of the local cream limestone. Just north of Oamaru is the Waitaki River, where Otago ends and Canterbury begins.

FORTROSE **The rich green pastures of Southland support the most intensive sheep farming in the world.**

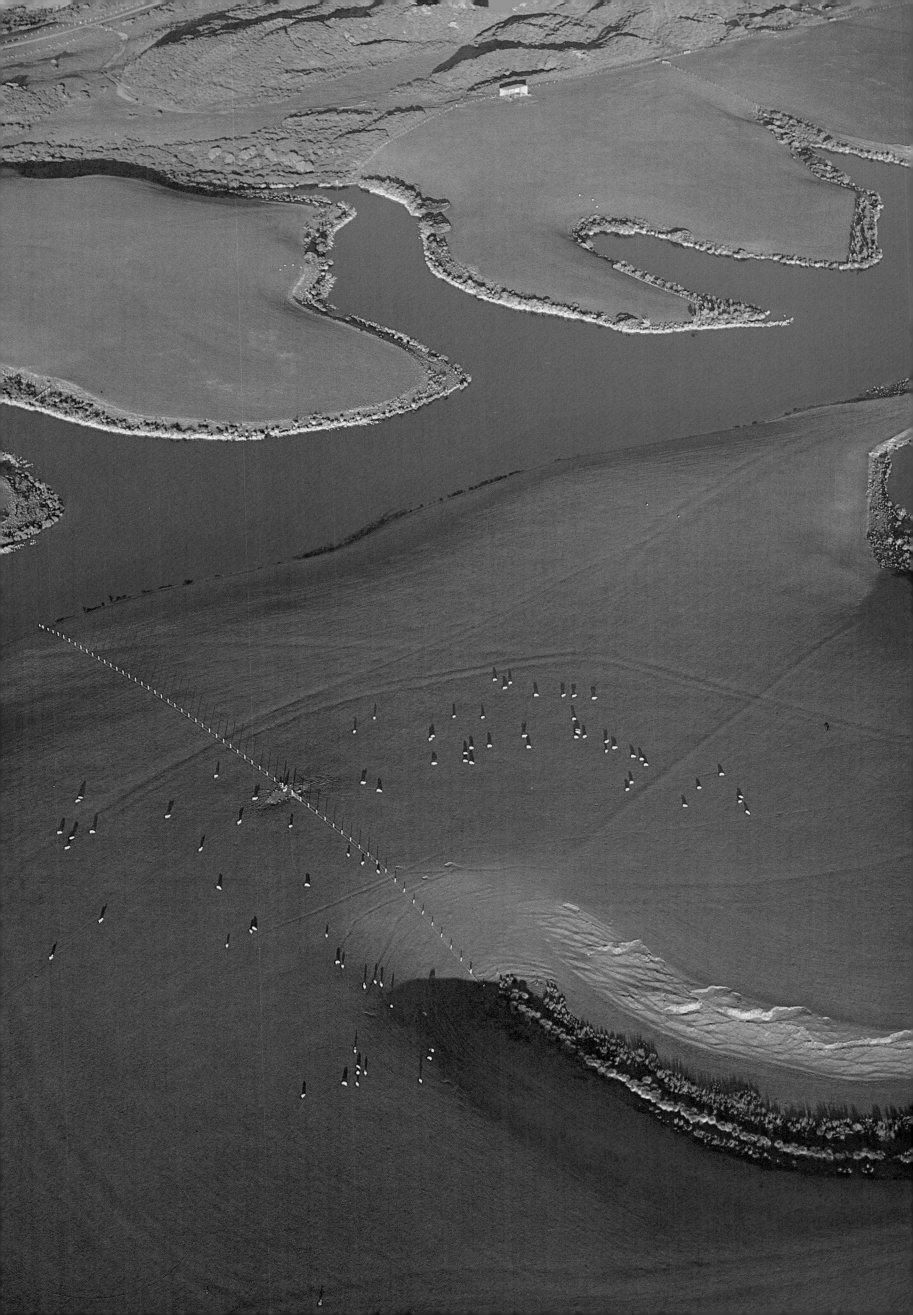

OBAN, STEWART ISLAND This island's one little town, which is situated within Half Moon Bay, is founded on fishing and holidaymaking. Nearby are coves with sandy beaches that are ideal for swimming and that attract many visitors every year. To explore the island's unspoiled shoreline, the visitor must walk.

ALUMINIUM SMELTER, TIWAI POINT Bauxite is shipped from Australia to New Zealand and is processed here, using hydro electric power that is generated at Lake Manapouri. Most of the aluminium is sent overseas from Bluff Harbour. Beyond Bluff Harbour, Stewart Island rises on the skyline.

INVERCARGILL At the foot of the South Island, this is the most southerly city in New Zealand. As its latitude is almost 48 degrees south, the climate is subantarctic. The chief city of Southland is flat and featureless, with wide streets and many reserves. The main one, Queens Park (foreground), caters to a variety of active and passive recreation, with its sports grounds and gardens.

Left: TE WAEWAE BAY This huge bay is open to stormy weather, which usually comes from the south, giving the trees along the coastal frontage a permanent lean. The beach is a favourite hunting ground for the much prized shellfish, the toheroa.

RUAPUKE ISLAND, FOVEAUX STRAIT From this low, swampy island at the entrance to the strait, the Maori chief Tuhawaiki controlled most of the South Island to North Canterbury. He negotiated the sale of the Otago block in 1844. The island is now farmed by its Maori owners.

SWAMPLANDS Much of the coastal land on either side of Invercargill is swampy. A view west over the Waituna Lagoon towards Tiwai Point and Bluff Hill. Bluff Harbour handles Southland's largest exports of meat and wool.

THE NECK, PATERSON INLET **A view north towards the Muttonbird Islands from the entrance to Stewart Island's main harbour, on the western side of the island. A narrow peninsula, The Neck, was the site of a very early European settlement.**

WAITUNA LAGOON **Waituna Creek—the Maori name means 'stream of eels'—drains the low-lying plains east of Invercargill. It empties into this lagoon, which is etched by its meandering paths.**

WAIPAPA POINT The eastern end of the south coast was a notorious graveyard for ships. New Zealand's second worst shipwreck occurred here when in 1881, the *Tararua* was wrecked with the loss of over 130 lives. As a result, the Waipapa Point lighthouse was built.

BROTHERS POINT AND WAIKAWA HARBOUR This area is a lonely outreach of the little known Catlins wilderness area, between the Clutha and Mataura Rivers. The Catlins area has very varied scenery, which includes rivers, dense rainforest reserves, secluded bays and beaches, towering cliffs and windswept headlands. Waikawa harbour is the setting for a small farming community.

CURIO BAY FOSSIL FOREST **On the rock shelf at the left of the photograph, the sea has uncovered fossilised trunks and stumps of ancient trees related to the kauri and the Norfolk Island pine. These are visible at low tide, and it is thought that they were smothered by a volcanic eruption at least 160 million years ago. Other areas of the Catlins are well-known for archaeological discoveries; it is thought that the giant moa survived longest here.**

Over: FORTROSE, TOETOES HARBOUR **This little settlement, on the edge of the Mataura River estuary, was the site of a whaling station established by Tommy Chasland in 1834. Whalers named the harbour and bay after the Maori chief, Toitoi.**

BALCLUTHA **The name of the town proclaims its Scottish origins—it is Gaelic for 'town on the Clutha', New Zealand's largest river. Balclutha is the main town for a large farming area of South Otago.**

OPEN CAST MINE, KAITANGATA **High-quality coal that lies in deep seams here has been mined either above or below ground for more than a hundred years. Decreased demand for coal in recent times has reduced the mine's output.**

STORM OVER THE CATLINS RIVER **Farmland has been wrested from the forest on one of New Zealand's last pioneering frontiers. In this area, small farms did not flourish, townships have disappeared or been reduced to a few small dwellings. Most of the remaining forest is protected from indiscriminate logging.**

Right: CLUTHA RIVER MOUTH **This is the outlet for the river that carries a greater volume of water than any other in New Zealand. It makes its seaward way south-east. In this picture, the flat and fertile island of Inchclutha is on the left and the floodbanks are on the right.**

APRICOT ORCHARD, CROMWELL GORGE Apricots and other stone fruits grow particularly well in the Central Otago climate of extremes. However, many orchards along the narrow shelf of the Cromwell Gorge will be flooded after the construction of hydro dams along the Clutha River.

ALEXANDRA The Clutha River was extensively dredged for gold here in the 1890s, leaving an expanse of arid grey tailings (foreground). Gold today is seen in the autumn colours of the Lombardy poplars that fringe the many fruit orchards dotted through the area.

LAWRENCE **This quiet country town on the edge of Central Otago burst into existence after the discovery of gold at nearby Gabriel's Gully. In 1861, it had a larger population than Dunedin.**

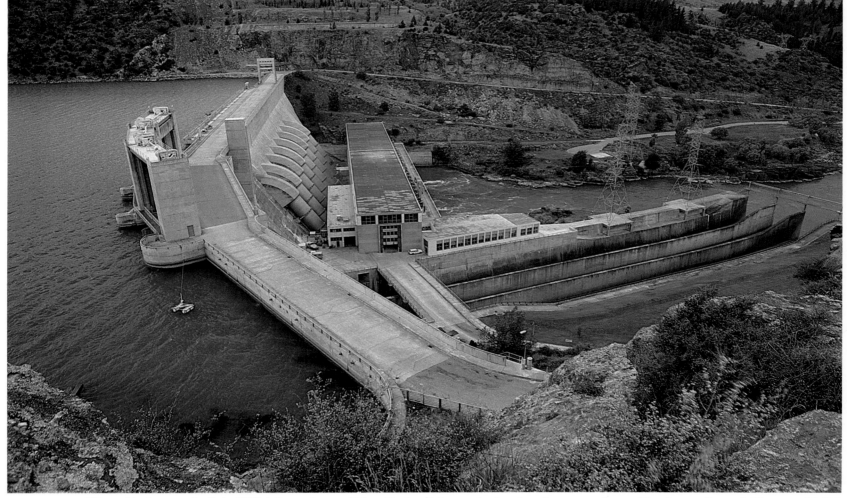

ROXBURGH DAM **When this dam was built in 1962, it formed part of New Zealand's largest hydro-electric power scheme. The dam wall stands 76 metres high. It was the first major project to harness the huge power potential of the Clutha.**

LAKE WANAKA **One of the major sources of the Clutha River, this lake has been carved out by glaciers. They also smoothed the surrounding hills before retreating to the mountains in the west. The Clutha winds out of the southern end of the lake to meet the Hawea River. Mount Aspiring, reflected in the glistening water, soars above the intervening ranges. The 3035-metre-high mountain gives its name to the surrounding National Park.**

GLENDHU BAY **A favourite spot for campers, Glendhu Bay is 13 kilometres to the west of the town of Wanaka. Willow trees in their autumn colours are reflected in the tranquil waters of Lake Wanaka, a popular spot for boating and fishing.**

THE OCTAGON, DUNEDIN **This eight-sided plaza at the heart of the city has its form accentuated by the encircling Moray Place. Looking from St Paul's Anglican Cathedral and the Town Hall, towards the railway station and the narrow harbour.**

SOUTH COAST FROM BLACK HEAD **These dramatic cliffs, which are pitted with tunnels and blowholes, are pounded by the Pacific swell. In the distance is St Clair, a suburb of Dunedin, and the Otago Peninsula.**

PORT CHALMERS **This is the deep water port of Dunedin, snugly nestled against the hills of Otago Harbour. It is watched over by the tall stone spire of the Iona Church.**

STUART STREET TERRACES **Dunedin's special character is largely a product of its fine Victorian architecture. This is a legacy of the commercial prosperity that followed the discovery of gold in the 1860s.**

DUNEDIN RAILWAY STATION **The self-confidence of Victorian Dunedin achieved its ultimate expression in this grand entrance to the city, built of local stone in 1904. Architect G. Troup was called 'Gingerbread George'.**

KARITANE **This picturesque seaside town at the Waikouaiti estuary mouth faces the volcanic Huriawa Peninsula, an ideal pa site. Sir Truby King founded the Plunket Society, which dramatically reduced infant mortality, from his home on the Karitane peninsula.**

NEW ZEALAND'S OLDEST FARM BUILDINGS, MATANAKA **Johnny Jones,** a colourful character in the early nineteenth century, established this farming settlement at the northern end of Waikouaiti Bay in 1839 after a prosperous career as a whaler.

OTAKOU MARAE **This is a modern church and meeting house at the settlement on the Otago Peninsula that gave the province its name. Otakou means 'red earth'. In the burial ground behind the church are the graves of several South Island chiefs.**

Right: LARNACH CASTLE **Superbly situated on the Otago Peninsula and built of the best imported materials, this castle was the dream of W. J. Larnach. He was a banker who became Colonial Treasurer in 1877. The grandiose mansion was described as 'doubtless the most princely . . . residence in New Zealand.' Larnach lost a great deal of money when his bank failed in the 1890s and he shot himself at Parliament Buildings, Wellington, in 1898.**

MOERAKI BOULDERS **According to Maori legend, these rocks were food baskets that were washed ashore when an ancestral canoe was wrecked. Geologists have explained that they are septarian boulders formed on the sea floor about 60 million years ago. They have been eroded from the soft mudstone cliffs of this North Otago beach. Many of the smaller boulders have been removed but those that remain are protected.**

KAKANUI MARKET GARDENS **Kakanui is a fertile district south of Oamaru, noted for its tasty tomatoes. The coast and estuary here are also very popular places for holidays. Oamaru itself, the second most populous place in Otago, is a centre for agriculture and sheep farming.**

LIMESTONE QUARRY, OAMARU The cream sandstone formed in thick vertical beds has been cut into blocks and used on many impressive buildings in New Zealand. The sandstone is soft enough to be easily sawn, but hardens with exposure.

OAMARU STONE BUILDINGS The local stone has given an architectural distinction to the town of Oamaru. The intricately carved Corinthian columns of the bank buildings have withstood the effects of the weather for over a century.

Canterbury

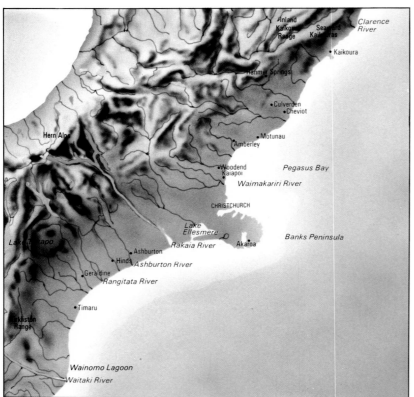

Most of Canterbury's coastline is a smooth, sweeping edge to the vast plains formed by shingle and silt washed down from the Southern Alps. The shape of the province is very clear from the air. Away to the west are the snow peaks of the long Alpine Range, then steep hill country that gives way to downlands reaching the coast at Timaru in the south and Waipara in the north. The Canterbury Plains enclosed between these points slope imperceptibly from the foothills to the Pacific Ocean. They are a mammoth patchwork quilt of fields in greens, browns and yellows, stitched together by hedgerows.

Before English colonists introduced their agricultural patterns, the Plains were all khaki tussock land, disconcertingly empty to the pilgrims who first viewed them after trudging up the hills from Lyttelton where their ships landed in 1850. Samuel Butler observed: 'The view was rather of the long stare variety. There was a great extent of country but very few objects to attract the eye. The Plains would have been wonderfully improved by an object or two a little nearer than the mountains.' The most obvious natural objects on the level expanse are the wide shingle beds of the braided rivers that have smoothed alluvium to form the Canterbury Plains.

The great sweep of Canterbury's coast is broken halfway along by the volcanic hills of Banks Peninsula, which was once an island.

Canterbury's southern border, the Waitaki, is the first of the rivers that fan out in parallel lines across the Plains. By digressing from our coastal track to follow the river to its source, we can appreciate the distinctive character of the Canterbury high country, so totally different from the coastal region. Where the hills start to rise from the plain, the Waitaki's wide riverbed narrows into a funnel of lakes and dams created to produce hydro-electric power. Further inland, the Waitaki breaks up into separate branches leading to the three glacial lakes that feed the river—Ohau, Pukaki and Tekapo. Remnants of the glaciers are visible towards the skyline, tucked into the folds of the Main Divide.

The high country was marked out for sheep stations by the Englishmen who came here first. The dominance of the sheep and the social structure of the Wakefield settlement have had a profound influence on Canterbury. Apart from the thinly scattered sheep and occasional homesteads, the high country has few signs of habitation. Awesome in its uncompromising emptiness, it is a powerful landscape of shingle slides on steep slopes and tussocks covering the more rounded ranges.

Back on the coast we continue our northern progression at Timaru, the main centre of South Canterbury. The city is built on gentle hills rising from a busy port. Its substantial homes, set in attractive gardens, reflect the solid prosperity of the surrounding countryside.

The plains between Timaru and Christchurch produce most of the country's wheat and other grain as well as the renowned Canterbury lamb. For many farmers, the biggest problem is drought. Fields soon become parched during the dry summer months, especially after a Norwester, the infamous Canterbury wind that is hot, dry and forceful. Irrigation schemes have reduced the disastrous effects of drought and helped preserve Canterbury's reputation as the best

mixed farming area in New Zealand.

Banks Peninsula forms a fascinating contrast to the surrounding lowlands. Its hills and harbours, valleys and bays are part of a volcanic landscape quite distinct from anything else in the South Island. Even the climate is different, with a rainfall twice that of the Plains. The rounded contours of the old lava flows, which protrude into a turquoise sea like plump toes, are separated by narrow bays. The largest indentations are the two craters that form Lyttelton and Akaroa harbours.

Akaroa township, charming and secluded on the south side of the Peninsula, carries echoes of its beginnings as a French settlement. In 1840 a party arrived in New Zealand from France to establish a colony there, only to find the British had beaten them. French influence survives in family and street names and in early architecture which has been preserved and enhanced by sensitive planning.

Lyttelton Harbour holds greater importance in the history of Canterbury. Its port was the main gateway to the South Island for a long time. Tucked between the wharves and the steep crater wall, Lyttelton township has all the salty atmosphere of an old maritime centre although it has adapted to container shipping and the end of the passenger link between the North and South Islands.

Christchurch, the South Island's largest city, sprawls over the plains just north of Banks Peninsula. It began as a planned Anglican settlement and is proud to be a southern bastion of Mother England. This pride shows among the loops of the quiet Avon River, the Gothic stone buildings, the deciduous trees and even in the way the people dress. They have been called smug and conservative, somewhat aloof from the rest of New Zealand. For all its size, Christchurch is predominantly a market town, serving the farming community on which its prosperity

depends. The annual Agricultural and Pastoral Show is a big occasion, a public holiday that town and country celebrate together. The city's strong civic pride has produced unequalled facilities such as the Town Hall, Commonwealth Games stadium, Arts Centre and the 200-hectare Hagley Park.

Christchurch is also fortunate in its beaches on a coast far more hospitable than that south of Banks Peninsula. From South Brighton by the estuary of the Avon and Heathcote Rivers, they curve away to the north in the grand sweep of Pegasus Bay. The surf, good for swimming, breaks onto an expanse of grey sand backed by rows of dunes.

At Kaiapoi on the mouth of the Waimakariri River are remnants of the river port that used to serve North Canterbury. The town takes its name from Kaiapohia Pa, a major fortress that was sacked by Te Rauparaha in 1831. Further on near Waipara the main road turns inland and the plains give way to low ranges and riverflats. The North Canterbury coast is left to grazing sheep on top of crumbling limestone cliffs.

Another of the many contrasts on the South Island's east coast appears as we approach the towering Kaikoura Ranges. The views can be magnificent and spectacular or menacing and hostile, depending on the moods of sky and sea. Jagged reefs and rocky outcrops are flailed by strands of kelp. Fishermen's cottages dot the narrow ledge between sea and cliff. The area is named after the crayfish (koura) which abound along this coast. There is a break in the rock-walled shoreline where a fertile plain reaches out to Kaikoura Peninsula. The former island has a seal colony on its outer edge and on the inland side sits Kaikoura township, dwarfed by its mountain backdrop.

CANTERBURY PLAIN SOUTH OF BANKS PENINSULA **The vast alluvial plain is cultivated to a ruler-straight, gravelled edge trimmed by the waves of the Pacific Ocean.**

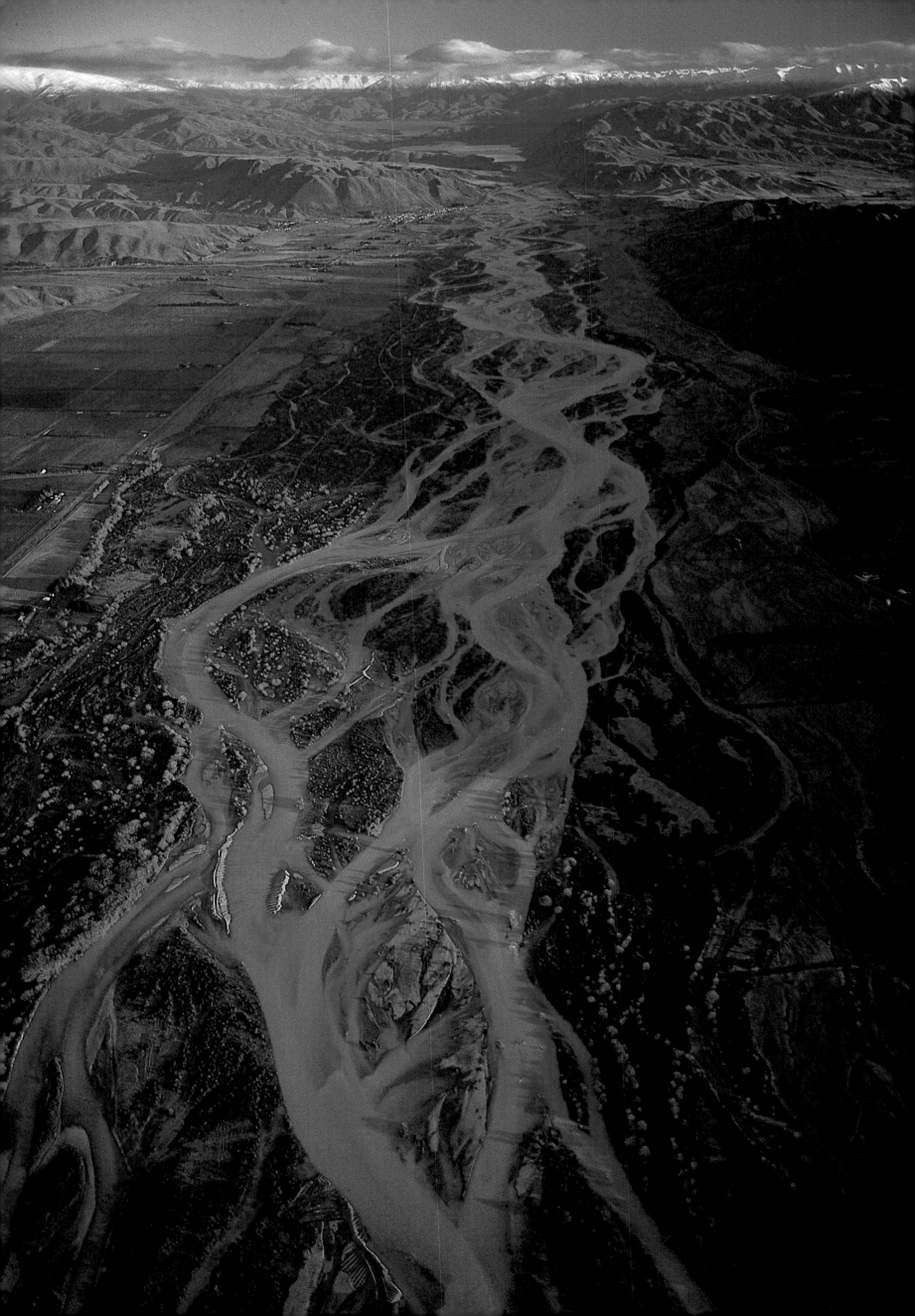

KIRKLISTON RANGE The soft pink tones of the rising sun spotlight the mountain ridge in the lower Waitaki catchment area. The Mackenzie Basin is in the distance.

BEN OHAU RANGE The snow-dusted mountains between Lakes Pukaki and Ohau, two of those that feed the Waitaki River, loom over a Mackenzie Country farm.

WAITAKI FISHING HUTS The settlement is a base for anglers after the quinnat salmon.

MACKENZIE BASIN This arid basin is framed by the Grampian Mountains (left) and the Dalgety Range (right), with Mount Cook piercing the clouds in the centre. The tussock land contained only remote sheep farms until the recent development of massive hydro schemes.

Left: WAITAKI RIVER Forming the boundary between Otago and Canterbury, this river starts in the snow-fed lakes of the Southern Alps and is dammed in the Upper Valley for power generation. Its braided streams then weave their way to the coast.

HALL RANGE **The steep barren slopes, part of the Southern Alps, are on the western side of the glaciated valley occupied by Lake Tekapo. Its milky turquoise waters are coloured by rock flour ground finely during glacial movement. Many other Canterbury lakes have a similar appearance.**

LAKE TEKAPO **A view across a larch plantation near Tekapo township. The trees provide some relief in the otherwise treeless tussock land of the Mackenzie Country.**

TEKAPO TOWNSHIP **A substantial tourist centre has grown up here since the development of skifields nearby. Part of its year-round appeal is the healthy, dry climate.**

Right: KIRKLISTON RANGE **These mountains form part of the principal watershed between the Hakateramea River and Lake Benmore. The clear light of an early morning frost highlights the rounded contours of the foothills and the dark shadow line of trees in the centre.**

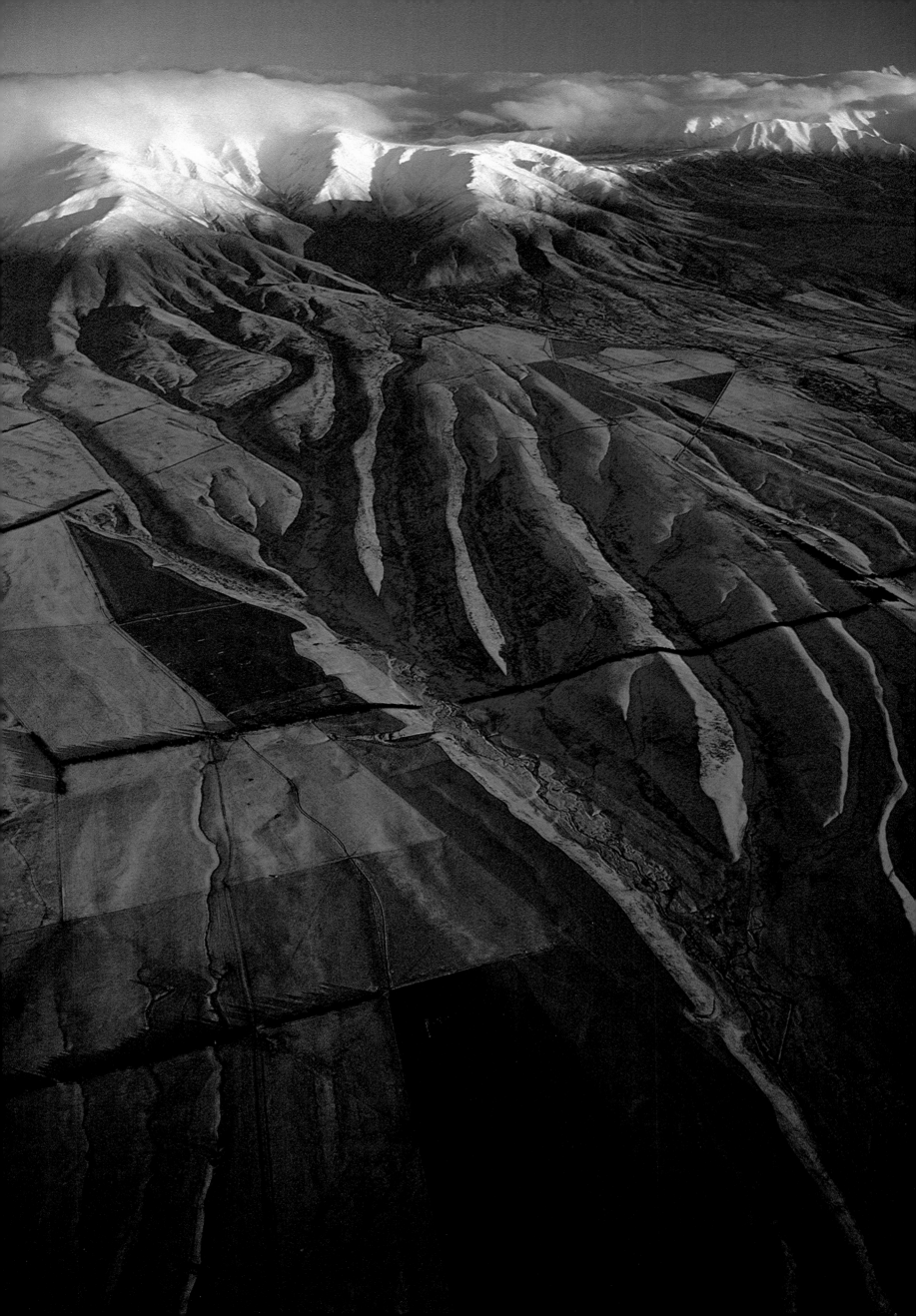

TUHAWAIKI POINT, SOUTH OF TIMARU **A ridge of basalt extending into the sea provides the only shelter on the South Canterbury coast and has made the construction of an artificial port possible. Timaru, the second city of Canterbury, serves a large farming district.**

TIMARU HARBOUR **Beyond the busy port is the English-style seaside resort of Caroline Bay. A carnival held here attracts crowds of holidaymakers each Christmas.**

Left: WAINOMO LAGOON **Halfway between the Waitaki River and Timaru, this lagoon is a wildlife refuge, wintering place for South Island geese that fly in from the high country valleys.**

Far left: COASTAL PLAIN NEAR WAITAKI **The plain has been built up with gravels and silt from the Alps, deposited by rivers.**

Over: RAKAIA RIVER MOUTH **The glistening streams of the wide river cut through this patchwork of agricultural land between Ashburton and Christchurch. The mouth is a favourite spot for salmon fishermen.**

HINDS RIVER **Irrigation of the area around Ashburton has transformed it from a bog into fertile land famous for its sheep and grain crops.**

PLOUGHING PATTERNS, SOUTH CANTERBURY **These fields prepared for spring planting may grow wheat, barley, oats or a vegetable crop.**

LONGBEACH HOMESTEAD **An autumn evening on an historic property on the Ashburton coast. The pioneer John Grigg developed Longbeach from a swamp to a showcase farm. The Queen and the Duke of Edinburgh stayed here during their first visit to New Zealand in 1953.**

MID CANTERBURY MOSAIC **The closely cropped fields north of Ashburton bear very little resemblance to the dry and gravelly plain that greeted the first settlers to the district. The man made landscape is laid out in a neat pattern of fields, reflecting the intensity and diversity of farming on the Canterbury lowlands. The plain produces most of New Zealand's grain but two-thirds of the land is in grass for livestock production.**

Gatefold over: GERALDINE **This picturesque area of rolling sheep country is situated between the southern Canterbury Plains and the higher land of the Four Peaks and the Mount Peel Ranges. The pastures were created out of forest and bush last century.**

BANKS PENINSULA **Lava flows created the fingers of land and sheltered harbours on the northern coast near Pigeon Bay. The peninsula was once an island volcano with twin craters that are now Lyttelton and Akaroa Harbours.**

AKAROA CEMETERY **On a hill above Akaroa Harbour, the resting place for the settlers who attempted to establish a French colony here in 1840. The first weeping willow introduced to New Zealand was brought to Akaroa.**

AKAROA **A quaint town tucked into the southeast of Banks Peninsula, it has an old world charm that attracts many visitors. There are still traces of its beginnings as the country's only French colony.**

Gatefold left: TIMARU DOWNS **A soft evening glow bathes the gentle hills around Timaru. In spite of a dry climate, this is a very fertile and prosperous district. Its wealth comes mainly from the famous Canterbury lamb, fattened on pastures like these and exported as frozen meat through Timaru's port. The land was first stocked with sheep in 1851 when the Rhodes brothers established their huge station, 'The Levels'.**

SUMNER HEAD **Looking across a steep escarpment on the edge of Banks Peninsula to where the Canterbury plains have spread down from the Alps to join the former volcanic island. In the foreground is the entrance to Taylors Mistake and beyond are the residential areas of Sumner and Clifton.**

LYTTELTON Encircled by the rim of an old volcano crater, Lyttelton is Canterbury's main port and the sea entrance to Christchurch. It was originally proposed as the site for the capital of the Canterbury settlement, but after the 'pilgrims' arrived in 1850, they crossed the Port Hills to establish themselves in Christchurch. A rail tunnel was completed in 1867, but it was another century before a road tunnel linked Christchurch with its port.

CYCLISTS, HAGLEY PARK Christchurch is ideal for cyclists because of its flatness. Tracks through Hagley Park link the northern suburbs and the city.

GOLDEN CARPET, HAGLEY PARK **Brilliant autumn colours are a sign of the sharp seasonal changes in Christchurch. One of the city's greatest assets is the 200-hectare park at its centre with hundreds of English trees bordering its playing fields, planted in the early years of settlement.**

THE ESTUARY **The view past Sumner's Cave Rock, a large deposit of volcanic lava, to the sandspit of South Brighton. The tidal estuary on the far side is rich in bird and marine life, and a popular spot for small boats and yachts. Christchurch's two rivers, the Avon and the Heathcote, unite here before being swallowed by the surf of the Pacific Ocean.**

BOTANIC GARDENS, CHRISTCHURCH **The gardens are enclosed within a loop of the Avon River in a corner of Hagley Park. There are two incursions into the otherwise sacrosanct green space of the park — the Public Hospital (top right) and Christ's College (centre). Between them is the old University of Canterbury, now an arts centre, and further in the distance a cluster of taller buildings marks Christchurch's civic and commercial centre.**

MOTUNAU BEACH, NORTH CANTERBURY **A fishing and holiday village on the south bank of the Motunau River and a great hunting ground for fossils along the cliffs. In 1962, a Canterbury schoolteacher made an important find when she discovered the fossilised remains of an extinct bony-toothed bird.**

HILLS FOR SHEEP **As the plains merge into the North Canterbury ranges, the main road turns inland and the coast, with its limestone cliffs, is left to the sheep. Wool and meat are the backbone of North Canterbury farming.**

HANMER SPRINGS FOREST **A wide variety of exotic trees have been planted in the State Forest. Its 7000 hectares are used for timber production and recreation. The fungi,** *Amanita muscaria,* **are attractive to look at but poisonous to eat.**

Over: RAINBOW **An early morning autumn shower casts a purple hue over the flat sheep paddocks and foothills near Culverden, north Canterbury.**

PARITITAHI TUNNEL, KAIKOURA **The Seaward Kaikoura Range drops steeply into the sea, producing a dramatically rugged coastline. On either side of Kaikoura township, the Christchurch-Blenheim road and rail line have had to be tunnelled through the base of the mountains in several places. The Parititahi tunnel is 11 kilometres south of Kaikoura.**

WAIAU BLUFFS **The layered structure of the land beneath the riverflats north of Waiau is unmasked by the sea. Most of this district was part of the Cheviot Estate, broken up by the government in 1892.**

MILKY SEA **Crumbling limestone cliffs eroded by sea and weather colour the water south of the Hurunui River. The north Canterbury shoreline between the Waipara River and the Kaikoura Coast is seldom seen by the traveller. The only beach settlements are Motunau and Gore Bay.**

KAIKOURA PENINSULA **This peninsula was once an island but is now tied to the mainland by the plain formed of debris from the Seaward Kaikoura Range. On the neck of the peninsula is the town and port (centre) and on the rocky outcrops is a large fur seal colony.**

KAIKOURA TOWNSHIP **Kaikoura is a Maori word meaning 'to eat crayfish', and the town is still best known for these crustaceans. It is also the centre for the dairying plains at the foot of the mountains.**

CHEESE MANUFACTURE **Separating the curds from the whey during the process of making cheddar cheese in the small Kaikoura factory. Cheese making is one of the area's principal industries; the country between the coast and the Seaward Kaikouras is flat and very suitable for dairying.**

Marlborough, Nelson

The surprising thing about the northern end of the South Island is how few people live there—only 3 per cent of New Zealand's population. The climate is warm and sunny, the scenery beautiful and varied. There are vast uninhabited tracts of bush-fringed, golden sand beaches beside a clear blue sea and fertile valleys between rows of impressive mountains. A spectacular maze of waterways and hills lies in the drowned valley system of the Marlborough Sounds.

Moa hunter and later Maori settlements were concentrated on the northeast coast of the South Island. The area was invaded by successive tribes from the North Island, but the Maori population was small when European settlers arrived. Nelson was the first planned settlement in the South Island, but never became more than a secondary centre. The smallness of the population is part of the region's appeal, allowing the visitor to appreciate its relatively unspoilt beauty and tranquillity.

The final stage in our aerial circumnavigation of the South Island continues along the Kaikoura coastline. The wild and rocky shore encountered south of the Kaikoura lowlands reappears to the north. After passing the tongue of land pushed out by the Clarence River, the coastline softens and displays fluted formations of eroded limestone. Imposing homesteads appear among rumpled treeless hills on which sheep graze—wool is the main product of Marlborough. Some very large sheep stations exist inland; the first in the South Island was Flaxbourne on the coast near Cape Campbell, the island's most easterly point. It was stocked with 3000 sheep shipped across from Sydney in 1847.

Once past the lighthouse at Cape Campbell, we have entered Cook Strait, where the Pacific and Tasman Oceans meet in the storm-tossed waters between the North and South Islands. Glistening white pyramids attract the eye west of the Cape to Lake Grassmere. On closer inspection they are revealed as enormous piles of salt harvested from the sea.

The most fertile area of Marlborough is the plain formed by the Wairau River where the provincial capital, Blenheim, is a focal point. A fraudulent claim to this land by settlers spilling over from the Nelson colony led to the only armed confrontation between Maori and pakeha in the South Island. After the government purchased the land in 1847 it was opened up for grazing. Today's mixed farming produces crops ranging from cereals and seeds to vegetables and flowers. An increasingly large area is being taken over for vineyards that thrive in the climate of low rainfall and plentiful sunshine. Blenheim has the greatest number of sunshine hours in the country.

Marlborough's other main town is Picton, nestled at the head of the Queen Charlotte Sound. It is an important transport terminal, providing berths for the freight and passenger ferries from Wellington operated by the Railways Corporation, yet it has retained its placid calm as a picturesque holiday town from which launches explore the labyrinth of bays, inlets and islands along the twisted shoreline of the Sound.

Captain Cook's *Endeavour* was the first ship to enter the Sounds in 1770. Queen Charlotte Sound so delighted the English navigator that he used it as a base for his New Zealand expeditions. Ship Cove, wreathed in variegated green bush and ringing with the pure song of the bellbird, looks today much as it would have looked then, except for a monument on the beach that commemorates Cook's five visits to the cove. While climbing a hill opposite, Cook first saw the strait that bears his name.

The next Europeans to arrive were the whalers, who established themselves near the bleak entrance to Tory Channel where the inter-island ferries now come and go. A whaling station was still operating here until the 1960s.

Attempts to farm the steep land between the fingers of water have not always been successful and have left many of the hillsides scarred. In parts, the natural cover is being allowed to regenerate as the recreational and scenic value of the Sounds is more widely appreciated. One of the most attractive areas still forested is Kenepuru Sound. It adjoins Pelorus Sound where a new type of farming is being established—growing mussels.

After passing the remote waterways and islands in the northwest of the Marlborough Sounds, we enter Tasman Bay and Nelson province. The city of Nelson is situated at the base of the U-shaped bay, protected by high hills on three sides and facing north to take full advantage of the region's abundant sunshine. Nelson has the distinction of being the first place in New Zealand to be given city status, although it is still a moderate sized provincial centre.

Following the tidal flats along the western side of Tasman Bay, we pass the well ordered patterns of the region's specialised crops — apples, hops and tobacco. The beaches are stunningly beautiful. They start near the city at Tahunanui but the most popular is Kaiteriteri where the sand becomes an orange-gold colour, the water is crystal clear and bush-covered islands and headlands give shelter. Beaches like this wind through to Abel Tasman National Park where there are no roads, only coastal walks for trampers.

Abel Tasman attempted to come ashore in December 1642 near the Tata Islands at the northern end of the park. One of his boats was attacked by Maoris and four crew members killed. Tasman sailed away, naming the place Murderers Bay and never set foot upon the land that he was the first European to discover.

A brighter episode in the story of Murderers Bay provided an opportunity to change its name to Golden Bay. This was the early gold rush that followed a find near Collingwood in the 1850s. Today the cleared lowlands of this remote corner are farmed but the forested hinterland has remained largely untouched. Untouched too is the long thin line of Farewell Spit that curls across the top of the Bay. It is formed of white quartz sand swept from the West Coast by strong sea currents. On its sheltered mudflats hordes of godwits gather in the autumn before setting out on their long journey to Siberia. The most northerly point of the South Island was also where Captain Cook farewelled the country after his first visit in 1770.

MARLBOROUGH SOUNDS **A remarkable maze of hills and waterways formed when the complex valley system of the South Island's northeastern corner was submerged and the sea snaked between the hilltops.**

CLARENCE RIVER Emerging from the valley (top left) that separates the Inland and Seaward Kaikoura Ranges, the Clarence River follows an earthquake fault line that is a branch of the great Alpine Fault.

KEKERENGU Both the road and the railway line skirt the coast north of the Clarence River where the fault line crosses Cook Strait to reappear as the West Wairarapa Fault.

Left: LIMESTONE RIDGE South of Cape Campbell, the southern portal of Cook Strait, the hills are low with a certain delicacy of contour that is often characteristic of limestone hills. They provide a marked contrast with the rugged range of the turbulent Kaikoura coast further south. Whitish in colour, limestone wears quickly.

Right: LAKE GRASSMERE SALTWORKS These are situated in a shallow lagoon where the high sunshine hours, low rainfall and strong dry winds provide ideal conditions for the production of salt from the sea by solar evaporation. Grassmere's annual output of 55 000 tonnes meets all of New Zealand's domestic and industrial salt requirements.

BLENHEIM **Seymour Square is the geometric heart of Marlborough province and New Zealand's sunniest spot. The circular building opposite the clock tower is the Borough Council's new administration centre, symbolising the town's rapid post-war growth.**

WAIRAU BAR MOA HUNTER SITE **This lonely farm on the Boulder bank at the outlet of the Wairau River produced a most exciting archaeological discovery — a moa hunter burial site that greatly increased knowledge of New Zealand's oldest culture. The moas, huge flightless birds that are now extinct, were chased down to the coast where they became trapped in the mud.**

DUAL BRIDGE, SEDDON **This highly unusual two-level bridge marks the northern approach to the small township of Seddon across the Awatere River. Road traffic uses the lower level and the upper level is a railway bridge. The town is named after a former NZ Prime Minister.**

WHITE BLUFFS, HAUTAKI **A dazzling sight between the Wairau and Awatere river mouths, these bluffs not far from the small town of Blenheim dramatically illustrate where the steep but soft limestone has been sharply sculpted by the forces of erosion over thousands of years.**

Over: TORY CHANNEL **The main sea link between Picton and Wellington separates Arapawa Island (foreground) and the northeastern tip of the mainland. Before the hilltops were denuded of their forest cover, Tory Channel was the base for whaling operations which continued until 1964.**

PICTON HARBOUR **A glorious setting for the South Island terminal of the inter-island ferry service that crosses Cook Strait from Wellington. Picton is the starting point for holidaymakers who wish to explore Queen Charlotte Sound.**

MUSSEL FARMING, PELORUS SOUND **Harvesting the shellfish from ropes attached to buoys began when it was thought that mussel extract was a cure for arthritis. However, they are now mainly sold as a delicacy.**

Left: ENDEAVOUR INLET **Clear blue waters are sheltered in the largest arm of Queen Charlotte Sound. Captain Cook used nearby Ship Cove as his base for careening his vessel and for exploration. The Inlet is 8.5 kilometres long.**

FRENCH PASS SETTLEMENT **Adjacent to the sheltered harbour, a turbulent current sweeps through the narrow strait that separates the mainland from D'Urville Island, the largest of the outer islands in Marlborough Sound.**

STEPHENS ISLAND **The northernmost tip of the Sounds, this steep cliffed island is home to lighthouse keepers and to rare wildlife such as the tuatara and the Stephens Island frog. Access to the lighthouse is difficult, as there is no landing place for boats. Passengers and goods have to be hauled up onto the island.**

PELORUS SOUND TO TASMAN BAY **From high above Tawhitinui Reach and Croisilles Harbour (top left), an evening vista across the calm waters of Tasman Bay.**

Left: WESTERN SOUNDS **A view from the numerous bays of Croisilles Harbour (foreground) across the mainland to the Chetwode Islands (top left) and Titi Island (top right). It is often difficult to distinguish islands from the mainland.**

ATAWHAI AND NELSON HAVEN **Suburban houses on the port hills above the placid Haven on the northern outskirts of the city with one of the most favoured situations and climates in the country.**

HARDY STREET NELSON **The provincial centre has achieved a successful balance between economic growth and the preservation of a pleasant and relaxed way of life.**

BOULDER BANK **This natural breakwater at Nelson Haven almost encloses the reclaimed land of Port Nelson. Newer residential areas spread towards the tidal Waimea Inlet (top right). Boulder Bank is a bank of rocks that have eroded from cliffs and been moved by the tide to stretch out in a line for a distance of fully 13 kilometres.**

Right: NELSON CITY **The first in the country to be given city status, which was bestowed along with a bishopric in 1858. A prominent city landmark is Christ Church Cathedral (centre) on its tree-studded hill. Nelson city is enclosed by hills on all sides except the north. The area's economy depends on primary produce, particularly hops, fruit, dairying and sheep raising.**

HOP CROP, RIWAKA **Drying kilns and wired vines are a feature of the Motueka district which supplies hops to all the country's breweries. During the 1960s, a growing demand for seedless hops to produce high-quality lager beers changed the type of hop grown in the Nelson area, and the beer is now exported throughout the world. Tobacco is also grown in the area.**

GORSE **Introduced for fencing and shelter, the plant has become a pest. Its golden flowers blaze over whole hillsides.**

POTTERY, BRIGHTWATER **The Nelson area has attracted a strong community of artists and craftsmen, including many potters who utilise the high quality local clays. Here Peter Gibb works his pots in the Omaio pottery.**

APPLE ORCHARDS **An attractive texture created by the contoured lines of regimented fruit trees in New Zealand's main apple growing area. A substantial portion of Nelson's apple harvest is exported, as are other crops of the region.**

LOW TIDE **A pocket settlement in the southwest corner of Tasman Bay, bounded by the mudflats of a tidal lagoon.**

Over: TOTARANUI **Headquarters of the exquisite Abel Tasman National Park, established in 1942. The park is rimmed by dazzling orange beaches and offers unequalled coastal walks through its beech forests.**

TATA BEACH **One of the many spots in Golden Bay suitable for boating, fishing and swimming in idyllic surroundings with no fear of being crowded out by tourists or holiday makers.**

Left: NEAR TORRENT BAY, ABEL TASMAN PARK **The afternoon sun spotlights the shallow waters of a secluded cove on Tasman Bay. Abel Tasman Park is the smallest National Park.**

HISTORIC TATA ISLANDS **Abel Tasman moored his ships here in December 1642 and lost four crew members after the first encounter between Maori and pakeha. The Tata Islands are small islets about 800 metres offshore from Tata Beach in the southeastern corner of Golden Bay.**

FAREWELL SPIT The northwestern tip of the South Island is formed of quartz sandstone from the West Coast, deposited by sea currents in a curving bar. Its dunes and tidal flats are a refuge for many migratory wading birds. There is a theory that, if the sea level were lower, the North and South Islands would be linked by the extension of Farewell Spit.

Bay of Plenty, East Cape

East Cape is the first place in the world to receive the early morning rays of the sun. It is also the site of the first European landing in New Zealand; Captain Cook's historic footprints marked the sand near Gisborne in 1769. Here too in the East we start our aerial exploration of the North Island.

Cook's initial contact with the Maoris was less than friendly and, unable to obtain the provisions he needed, he named the place Poverty Bay. In contrast, the much larger Bay of Plenty was named by Captain Cook in recognition of a more successful visit. Here he found fertile cultivated land populated by a flourishing community. The name, Bay of Plenty, remains an apt description, unlike the totally inappropriate appellation, Poverty Bay.

The Bay of Plenty coast stretches in a great crescent of lovely white surf beaches from the Coromandel Peninsula to Cape Runaway in East Cape. Its natural boundaries are the Kaimai Ranges to the west and the Raukumara Range to the east. From the south, it is enclosed by the high country of the Ikawhenua Range and the Volcanic Plateau. Sheltered on all sides, the Bay looks north towards the warm Pacific Ocean. It enjoys a mild climate and is second only to Nelson, Marlborough in the hours of sunshine it averages.

The farms and orchards of the coastal belt produce dairy cattle, fat lambs and a wide range of sub tropical crops. The Bay of Plenty provides a large proportion of the country's citrus fruit (oranges, lemons and grapefruit). In recent times there has been a boom in exotic produce such as kiwifruit.

The Bay is part of the North Island's premier tourist region. Known as 'The Tourist Diamond', this area incorporates the beaches between Tauranga and Opotiki, the big game fishing grounds out to Mayor Island, the thermal region around Rotorua, and Lake Taupo in the centre of the island, famous for its trout fishing.

Our progress around the Bay of Plenty starts on the Coromandel boundary, where the coastal flat begins to broaden out. The low lying, pine forested Matakana Island forms a protective barrier between the sea and Tauranga Harbour, with the harbour entrance at its eastern end.

Looming over the other side of the harbour entrance is Mount Maunganui, once an island but now joined to the mainland by a narrow peninsula. Beneath the dominating presence of the flat topped cone lies Tauranga, an unusual combination of industrial port and holiday beach resort. Mount Maunganui's busy port handles a greater volume of exports than any other in the country. It has grown rapidly with the expansion of the forestry industry in the central North Island.

The city of Tauranga has also been transformed by post war development. Originally a mission station, Tauranga later became a military post, but the more peaceful times that followed saw it develop as a quiet farming and retirement centre. The boom in forestry and agriculture, brought about by improvements to the soil, has changed all that. It is now prosperous farming land with a concentration of attractive orchards around Tauranga.

Another attraction of the Bay is its fishing potential. The waters around Mayor Island are known to big game fishermen throughout the world for the sport offered by marlin, tuna and mako shark.

Across to the east lies another famous island. White Island is the most spectacular manifestation of the thermal activity that breaks through the earth's crust in this region. On the mainland, the best known thermal area is around Rotorua. This weird inferno features hot springs, boiling mud, hissing geysers — and the smell of rotten eggs. Last century, Rotorua developed as a spa where ailing people came to soak themselves in the mineral waters hoping for a cure. Visitors still flock here, but these days they enjoy a lot more than the hot pools.

Most of the Bay of Plenty consists of volcanic rocks and ash deposits. On the coast, sliced hillsides reveal pumice ash which was forced out of the largest crater of all — now Lake Taupo.

Just before leaving the Bay of Plenty for East Cape we come to Whakatane and its fine beach, Ohope. The town services surrounding farms, including those on the Rangitaiki Plains (once a swamp but now drained and transformed into fertile dairying country). Whakatane's main industry is a mill that turns pine logs into cardboard.

From the benign abundance of the Bay of Plenty we enter a wild terrain that has resisted man's efforts to tame it. East Cape, rugged, remote and sparsely populated, has an aura of untouchability which merges the past with the present.

The East Coast has a stronger Maori character than any other region. With over half the population Maori, their culture has remained more intact here than elsewhere. Most of the little settlements around the perimeter are centred on the marae, and the meeting houses are often finely decorated with examples of the art of carving which reached its peak in this area.

The rugged bluffs and headlands of the coastline are broken only by golden beaches unspoilt by the crass developments which have disfigured many northern beaches. In December, when the pohutukawa flowers are in crimson bloom, the coastline is particularly magnificent.

The stark ranges, which frequently reach to the sea, have been stripped bare. Once covered in forest, they suffered at the hands of the early European settlers. Indiscriminate burnoffs destroyed most of the natural vegetation, resulting in the most serious soil erosion in the country. Only in the interior does the original vegetation still thrive.

Most of the steep country that can be farmed is divided into large sheep stations. On the eastern side of the Cape, several townships display derelict remains of freezing works and wharves, a reminder that not so long ago, the only access to this area was by sea.

The one population centre of any size is Gisborne. This provincial city is situated at the junction of three rivers on the edge of the only substantial area of flat land on the East Coast. The fertile Gisborne Plain produces the bulk of the country's maize and a diversity of other crops. Vegetables including sweet corn, beans, peas and tomatoes are processed at a large cannery which has been a major boost to the local economy. Another rapidly growing industry is wine making, which capitalises on the plentiful sunshine of Poverty Bay.

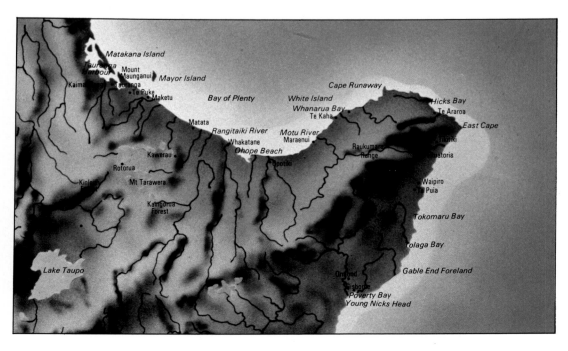

COOK'S COVE, TOLAGA BAY **Like much of the East Coast, the area has changed little since Cook's landing except for the removal of the bush.**

MT TARAWERA **The mountain, thought to be extinct, exploded without warning in 1886 in the most destructive volcanic eruption since European settlement. Three villages were buried and dozens of people killed.**

WHITE ISLAND **The most active and most northerly part of the Taupo-Rotorua Volcanic Zone, the island spurts a constant plume of white steam, marking its presence in the centre of the Bay of Plenty.**

Left: TAURANGA HARBOUR **A view from the outskirts of the city towards Mt Maunganui. Port and city have developed rapidly with the growth of the forestry industry and the recent expansion of farming and horticulture.**

THE SEAWARD SIDE OF MT MAUNGANUI **A very popular surfing beach. The flat Bay of Plenty coast curves gently from here to East Cape.**

BRAIN POT, ROTORUA **One of the geysers in the tourist village of Whakarewarewa shoots out of this hole at erratic intervals. It is reputed to have been used to cook the heads of enemies.**

MEETING HOUSE, TE KAHA **At the heart of each Maori community, the meeting house faces the open space of the marae where the people gather.**

VOLCANIC LANDSCAPE **An aerial view of one of the nine craters that opened when Mt Tarawera erupted in 1886, killing over 150 people. These volcanic deposits look very barren but are now beginning to support some vegetation.**

Left: LAKE ROTOMAHANA **Steam vents on the edge of the lake which was created by the Tarawera eruption. Thermal activity produces high water temperatures and colours the cliffs with deposits such as silica and sulphur.**

MAIZE NEAR MATATA **Fields of maize grown to provide supplementary feed for dairy cattle create attractive patterns when viewed from the air.**

SHELTERED ORCHARDS OF SUBTROPICAL FRUIT **High export prices from kiwifruit during the 1970s have brought prosperity to the Bay of Plenty area. Former dairy land is being planted in exotics such as passionfruit, tamarillos and avocados as well as kiwifruit and the longer established citrus fruits.**

RAUKUMARA RANGE **The difficult and precipitous terrain of East Cape has tended to discourage European settlement and has preserved the Maori identity of the region. Much of the interior is inaccessible.**

Left: MOTU RIVER **The western edge of the Raukumara Range meets the sea by the Motu River mouth — a magnificent stretch of coastal scenery.**

NEAR TE KAHA **A government supported co-operative enterprise is developing horticulture and fishing to encourage Maoris to return to the area. Wharekura Point in the centre of the bay is the site of a burial ground.**

Left: EXPOSED AND ROCKY COAST **Whaling was an important industry in the region east of Cape Runaway and there was a whaling station near here.**

CAPE RUNAWAY **The eastern corner of the Bay of Plenty, the Cape was named following an incident in which Captain Cook frightened away five canoes filled with Maoris. Grapeshot fired wide of them caused the warriors to 'run away' back to the headland.**

SUNRISE **The East Coast is the first place on the mainland (some claim in the Commonwealth) to receive the early morning rays of the sun.**

Left: THE LIGHTHOUSE AT EAST CAPE **The lighthouse was transferred from East Island which was considered too dangerous even for lighthouse keepers.**

Above: TOLAGA BAY **A layer of cloud trapped above one of the few pockets of flat land in the region of Tolaga Bay, 55 kilometres north of Gisborne.**

Over: ENTRANCE TO COOKS COVE, TOLAGA BAY **Cook described the two rocks: 'One is high and round like a cornstack, but the other is long with holes through it like the arches of a bridge'. His naturalist, Banks, declared it 'certainly the most magnificent surprise I have ever met with'.**

KUMARA HARVEST, POVERTY BAY **The kumara (sweet potato) was brought to New Zealand by Polynesian migrants and was a staple of their diet.**

Left: YOUNG NICKS HEAD, POVERTY BAY **The point was named after the surgeon's boy, Nicholas Young, who was the first member of the** *Endeavour's* **crew to sight land on 7 October 1769.**

Left: SHEEP MUSTER AT TATAPOURI NEAR GISBORNE **Many of the large hill stations of the Cape are still in the hands of Maori landowners.**

Above: RURAL PATCHWORK **A wide range of crops, from maize and vegetables to grapes and other fruit, is grown on the fertile plains of Poverty Bay.**

Preceding pages: GABLE END FORELAND **This dramatic cliff face is just north of Gisborne. Gilded in the early morning sun, it overwhelms the tiny lighthouse perched on its apex. The triangular shape of the cliff face reminded Captain Cook of the gable end of a house, and so he gave it its name.**

Hawkes Bay, Wairarapa

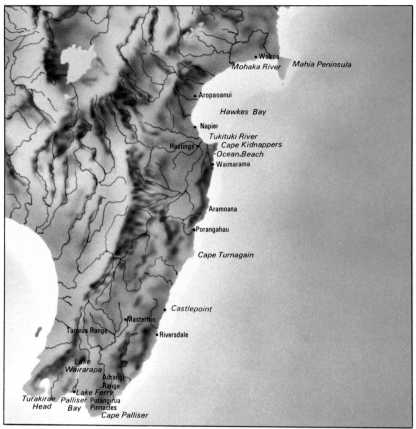

Most of the coast from Mahia Peninsula to Cape Turakirae on the southern tip of the North Island is little known to New Zealanders. The sheltered curve of Hawke Bay is familiar enough as the eastern boundary of the most fertile plains in the country. But the 350 kilometres south from Cape Kidnappers is cut off from the principal transport routes. Once the cities of Napier and Hastings are left behind, there are no significant settlements other than a few beach resorts, sparsely scattered considering the extent of this region. They are reached by side roads off the main trunk which is well inland.

The only feasible way to gain an overall appreciation of this stretch of coastline is by air. Some parts are inaccessible by any other means. Nearly all hill country, the landscape is vibrant green, speckled with the white dots of grazing sheep. Although the terrain varies as we travel southwards, it is mostly an irregular confusion of hills and gullies squeezed between the ranges on the west and the wild sea on the east. There are few trees apart from remnants of native forest in remote valleys and the odd plantation grown for shelter.

The Hawkes Bay, Wairarapa coast touches on some of the richest land in the country. Station homesteads stand out imposingly on the rolling pastures, suggesting permanence in a country where most man-made structures look temporary against the grandeur of the natural scenery. If New Zealand has an aristocracy it is most firmly rooted here, and in Canterbury, among family dynasties built on the backs of sheep.

The northern boundary of Hawkes Bay lies near Wairoa. Once a river port, its most distinctive feature now is a lighthouse (retired after service on the Mahia Peninsula) sitting oddly on a riverbank in the centre of the town. Nearby is the splendid Takitimu meeting house, a symbol of the Maori influence which is evident throughout the region, and particularly strong in the north.

Hawke Bay (the name of the Bay as distinct from the province) has a scalloped edge of vertical white cliffs. The hill country beyond becomes less broken to the south and gives way to the Heretaunga Plains that have been built up from the alluvial deposits of three main rivers — the Tutaekuri, the Ngaruroro and the Tukituki. The water they carry is funnelled into the Bay, irrigating the very productive plains that support fat lambs, crops, orchards and market gardens.

Hastings is the city at the centre of this activity. Often described as 'the fruit bowl of New Zealand', it could just as easily claim to be the country's vegetable basket. The output of a tremendous variety and quantity of vegetables has grown with the very successful canning industry founded by Sir James Wattie. Much of the fruit harvest, especially peaches, apples and pears also ends up in cans.

This, too, is the country's main wine making district. The benevolent climate of Hawkes Bay — high sunshine and low rainfall — is ideal for grape growing and wines of good quality are being produced.

The rivalry between Hastings and Napier is difficult for an outsider to appreciate. Although so close, each city jealously guards its own identity; yet they are interdependent. Hastings is the processing centre for agricultural and horticultural produce. Napier is the business and government centre, and has the only port in the region.

The Napier we see today was completely rebuilt after the disastrous earthquake of 1931. Parts of the new city are standing on the rubble of the old. Other parts are on land that was raised by the earth's convulsion — the site of the airport was previously a huge lagoon. This natural reclamation of 3200 hectares was the most positive outcome of the earthquake. Over all, it was the worst catastrophe in New Zealand's history. Two hundred and fifty-six people lost their lives, and the buildings that were not toppled were destroyed in a huge fire that started minutes after the first shake. Hastings was also devastated, and in other places the land changed its appearance. On the coast north of Napier, huge slips into the sea remain as legacies of the earthquake.

Napier has recovered remarkably. Industry has flourished; the Harbour Board, enriched by its gift of land from the sea, has developed a major port; and the city has built an image as a holiday centre. Although the climate is ideal, Napier's shingle beach is not suitable for swimming; instead, the beachfront boasts a parade of man-made attractions.

The rural wealth of Hawkes Bay and Wairarapa is reflected in many of the recreation activities. Hunt clubs, horse breeding and racing are very strong. There is also a concentration of private schools based on English models.

At the southern point of Hawke Bay is Cape Kidnappers, named by Captain Cook after an attempt by Maoris to seize a Tahitian boy from the *Endeavour*. The Cape's wedge shaped point jutting into the sea is a well known bird sanctuary, housing the only gannet colony sited on a mainland.

Travelling south from Cape Kidnappers, we come upon two fine surf beaches — Ocean and Waimarama. Further south, fewer people venture into the more turbulent waters; the sand shelves steeply where the powerful sea pushes it up against the cliffs. Man's footprints are harder to find as we move down the east coast.

Captain Cook turned his back on this part of the country soon after his first landfall. Having sailed south from Poverty Bay, he could find no sheltered anchorage and decided to retrace his steps. Cape Turnagain, where he changed direction, is a lonely promontory shared today by sheep and cabbage trees.

The next major bluff has a small settlement at its base. Castlepoint was named by Captain Cook on a later stage of his voyage because of the shape of the headland. These days, the beach below the headland is renowned for the horse races held on its sand each March. Opposite, on the seaward side of the lagoon, sits a lighthouse atop a rocky pillar, a reminder of the many shipwrecks along the treacherous coast. Castlepoint and Riversdale are the only beaches within easy reach of Masterton and the other main towns of the Wairarapa, which are all situated along an inland valley.

As we approach the south-east corner of the North Island, the rugged landscape reaches greater heights. The Aorangi mountain range rises steeply from the forbidding coast to a skyline of jumbled peaks. Then suddenly, as we pass Cape Palliser, the bleak prospect changes. The bay that is revealed was a favoured site for Maori settlement; there were birds and fish in abundance and kumara grew well. Rows of stones can still be seen marking the boundaries of Maori gardens.

Inland from Palliser Bay, past the shallow waters of Lake Wairarapa, is the rich farmland of the Ruamahanga Valley. It is flanked on the west by the Rimutaka Range — the boundary between Wairarapa and Wellington.

NAPIER'S MARINE PARADE **It was a narrow shingle spit leading to the city before the 1931 earthquake raised the land to the west.**

CLIFFS AT AROPAOANUI **Halfway round the bight of Hawke Bay, these cliffs display the effect of the violent upheaval in 1931. Huge chunks of the papa hills were sent slumping into the sea. Similar slips occurred inland but most of their scars are now healed.**

NORTHERN HAWKES BAY **The ranges, shorn of their forest cover to create sheep farms, have been prone to soil erosion.**

HUNTER AND FISHERMAN **If conditions at sea are not favourable for fishing, the locals hunt the game of the Mahia Peninsula.**

Above: EASTERN HAWKE BAY **Sunset casts a golden glow over the Whakaki Lagoon and low lying swampland near Wairoa.**

Over: NAPIER AIRPORT **Ahuriri Lagoon was raised up to two metres by the Hawkes Bay earthquake, creating the flat land on which Napier's airport now sits.**

HASTINGS At the centre of the rich farms and orchards of the Heretaunga Plains, the city is the home of a large food processing and canning industry. The streets of Hastings are arranged in neat blocks and numbered on the American system.

PUPILS OF WOODFORD HOUSE There are several private boarding schools in Hawkes Bay catering mainly for the daughters or sons of sheep farmers.

Left: VINEYARD NEAR MATAHIWI Hawkes Bay with its mild climate has built a reputation as the premier wine growing district in the country. The industry has grown rapidly to meet the increased local demand for its product.

Right: CAPE KIDNAPPERS Known to the Maoris as the fish hook of Maui, the Cape was renamed by Captain Cook after Maoris had attempted to kidnap one of his crew members here. The flat patches along the ridge are occupied by a famous gannet colony.

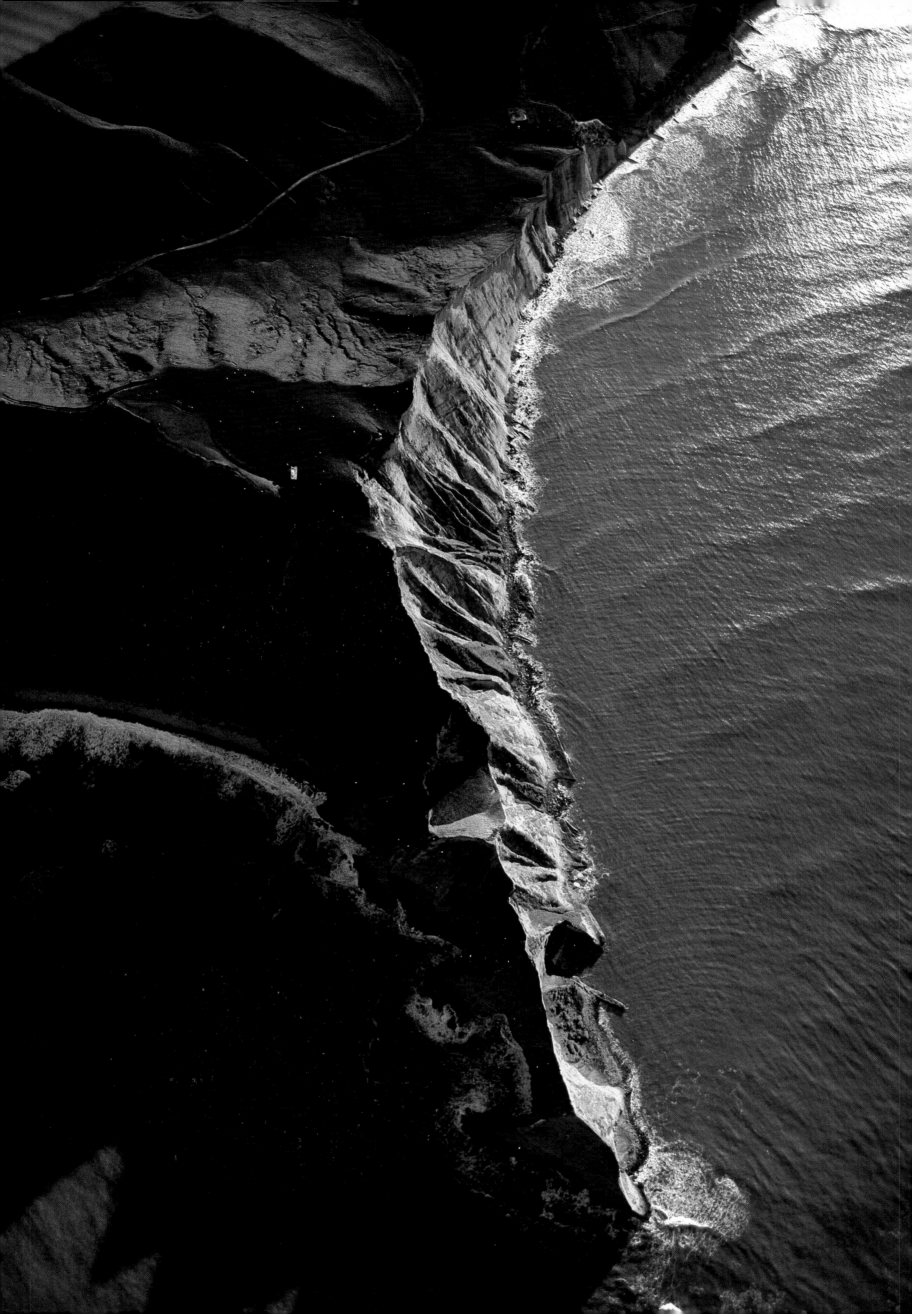

SOUTHERN HAWKE BAY The strata of sedimentary rocks are clearly revealed on these massive cliffs. A track along the beach below gives access to the gannet sanctuary at Cape Kidnappers if the tide is not too high.

Right: TUKITUKI RIVER **The river has deposited soil from the Ruahine Range to help create the central Hawkes Bay plains. When it was still surrounded by thick bush, the river was an important highway.**

BLACKHEAD **Holiday cottages nestle on the exposed beach by the mouth of the Porangahau River. Nearby is a scow wrecked in 1927.**

ARAMOANA, WAIRARAPA COAST **Until 1928 all stores had to be shipped in to this station homestead.**

Above: WHANGAEHU CLIFFS, WAIRARAPA **The gently rolling pasture land belies the wild ferocity to be found where land and sea abruptly clash. Sheep graze to the razor edge, unperturbed by their perilous position.**

Right: CAPE TURNAGAIN **The southern Wairarapa coast stretches into the distance. It was here that Captain Cook abandoned the course he had set, after his arrival in Poverty Bay, and turned to the north.**

CASTLEPOINT FOSSILISED SHELLS **These fossilised molluscs which have been exposed on the reef at Castlepoint form part of the geological calendar. They are from the Upper Pliocene period and are probably about four million years old.**

RIVERSDALE **A popular beach east of Masterton, it is the last one suitable for swimming, surfing and fishing before the south-east coast becomes increasingly hostile and inaccessible.**

WHAREAMA RIVER **This remote river valley between Castlepoint and Riversdale is typical of the Wairarapa area. Although the terrain may be very rugged in places, it is a particularly rich part of the North Island.**

Left: CASTLEPOINT **The curving reef, topped by a lighthouse, encompasses a quiet lagoon. Castlepoint was Wairarapa's main shipping outlet until the rail link with Wellington was built in the 1880s.**

WHATARANGI **Holiday houses on the windswept eastern shore of Palliser Bay. A road rises through the Aorangi Mountains to Haurangi Forest Park.**

CRAY FISHERMAN, NGAWIHI **The seas around Cape Palliser are a rich source of seafood.**

Left: BLACK ROCKS AT CAPE PALLISER **The North Island's most southerly point, Cape Palliser is lashed by the stormy seas of Cook Strait which have caused many wrecks in the area.**

SAILS OF KUPE **The first Polynesian voyager is said to have spread his sails to dry in Palliser Bay, leaving this imprint on the cliffs.**

Over: SOUTH WAIRARAPA **One of the first parts of the North Island to be farmed because of its lack of bush, the area is still comparatively isolated.**

PUTANGIRUA PINNACLES **Shingle hillsides on Cape Palliser have eroded unevenly, creating an impressive spectacle of cliffs and pillars. The pillars have remained standing where there are protective caps of resistant rock.**

LOWER RUAMAHANGA VALLEY **A swampy plain separates the sea and Lake Wairarapa. Further inland the valley holds the main population centres.**

Above: EARTHQUAKE CALENDAR Cape Turakirae at the western end of Palliser Bay has been uplifted by successive earthquakes. Each upheaval is marked by a raised beachline from the earliest at the foot of the hill, 6500 years old, to the most recent which was raised 2.5 metres in 1855.

Right: LAKE FERRY The lake forms the outlet for the Ruamahanga River. The hotel in the fishing settlement was originally licensed on the condition that the publican ferry travellers across the lake.

Wellington, Manawatu

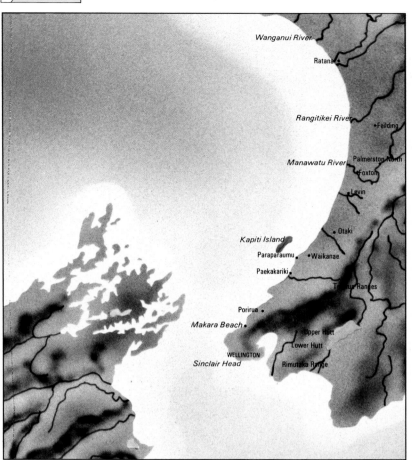

Where the North Island tapers to its end in Cook Strait, the land has been pushed up and twisted into a complex pattern of ridges and gullies. Along the short southern coast the hills draw apart to allow the sea in through a narrow entrance, a break in the circle of steep hills that embrace Wellington Harbour. More like a lake than a harbour, it has many moods, but on rare occasions when the sun is shining and the air is still, Wellington Harbour is breathtakingly beautiful.

Squeezed between the southern end of the harbour and the turbulent sea coast is the city of Wellington. It utilises its precious patch of flat land to the full. Office towers reach upwards from the largely reclaimed city centre while the residential areas spill over the hillsides into nearby valleys. It is an improbable site for a capital city. The aggressive terrain has a climate to match and the threat of earthquakes is ever present. Yet those features which outsiders scorn make possible the virtues appreciated by those who live there — the close knit city living and the spectacular setting.

The land traveller can only leave Wellington in one direction — northwards. He can either take the winding Rimutaka Hill road to Wairarapa or follow the main route along the west coast. On this road, the Tasman Sea is first revealed in a magnificent view from above Pukerua Bay. At first the coast is rocky and steep, then there are the sand dunes of the 'Gold Coast' beaches sweeping west. The buckled hill country to the south merges into the more ordered line of the Tararua Range. Between them and the sea the plains widen, reaching their full extent in Manawatu.

The sea approach to Wellington is made difficult enough by the notorious winds funnelled through Cook Strait. A further hazard is Barrett Reef at the harbour entrance. Among its victims was the inter island ferry *Wahine* which struck it during a violent storm in 1968. The ship sank and 51 people died. The ferry service between Wellington and Lyttleton ended soon after and now the only regular passenger link with the South Island terminates in Picton.

Many of the *Wahine* passengers were washed ashore on the rocks of the inhospitable eastern shore between Pencarrow and Eastbourne. The harbour is more welcoming further in. Bays where Wellingtonians used to holiday now contain expensive homes of diplomats and other city commuters.

At the northern end of the harbour is the valley of the Hutt River. At its mouth the first planned English settlement was started in 1840. The river's tendency to flood forced the colonists to shift to the present site of Wellington. Now the flooding is under control and, after several stages of development, the valley has become a large population centre. First the forest was milled, then market gardens flourished and since the 1930s housing and industry have taken over. Petone Borough on the foreshore and the cities of Lower and Upper Hutt, are linked to the capital by the busiest suburban railway in the country and a motorway that ends abruptly in the city.

Wellington still retains some of its Victorian flavour, particularly in the characteristic wooden houses that perch precariously on her slopes. But the old city centre is rapidly disappearing under the demands for office space from commercial and government Head Offices. Wellington has been the capital since

1865, when the seat of government was moved from Auckland to the geographically more central location. It is the most distinctively New Zealand city, as man has little chance of moulding it into some European model. Nature refuses to be subdued; deciduous trees and exotic plants that soften other cities have little effect against the sombre green native bush on the hilly backdrop.

Few Wellingtonians know the southern coast at their backs. From Owhiro Bay, the south-west butt of the North Island around to Porirua Harbour is glimpsed by travellers flying in or out of Wellington Airport. But otherwise it is familiar only to trampers, fishermen and the local farmers. The bare hills drop steeply into the sea with a narrow shingle ledge where the two meet. A tiny settlement at Makara has the only beach accessible by road.

The best beaches are further north. From Paekakariki to Waikanae, the temperature is usually several degrees warmer than in Wellington. On summer weekends many people escape from their hemmed in city to these expanses of sand dunes and surf. The area is known as the 'Gold Coast' or Kapiti Coast after the brooding island opposite Paraparaumu. Kapiti was the stronghold of the formidable Maori chief, Te Rauparaha who led far-reaching war parties from here, early last century. His remains share the island sanctuary with some of the rarer species of native birds. There is a memorial to Te Rauparaha opposite the beautiful Maori church at Otaki on the mainland. The church was built in 1849 when Otaki was the site of an influential mission station. Today, the town is known for its market gardens which, with those of Levin, supply fresh vegetables to Wellington.

As we continue our northward flight along the coast, the shape of Manawatu becomes clear. The broadening plains are intersected by a series of rivers which have their origins in the bleak ranges to the east. The seaward boundary is marked by sand dunes, on some of which are pine plantations to stop the sand encroaching on farmland.

The wealth of Manawatu is firmly based on agriculture. There is a balance of beef, dairy and sheep farming with some horticulture. The towns are all primarily servicing centres for the surrounding farmland, although there has been a certain amount of manufacturing development.

Foxton, at the mouth of the Manawatu River, seemed destined to be the main centre for the region. A thriving industry developed around the flax plants that grew naturally in the area, until, in the 1880s, there were 50 flax mills. Today they have gone, along with the port. The reason for Foxton's decline was that the main rail line was built from Wellington to Palmerston North, bypassing the coastal town and creating a new commercial hub inland. Palmerston North also had ready access to the east through the Manawatu Gorge.

The coastal plains end as we approach Wanganui and the lowland hills reach to the coast. Manawatu has the largest area of flat land in the North Island. It lacks the dramatic landscape found elsewhere, but has its own subdued interest — especially from the air.

Right: WELLINGTON HOUSES **From the slopes of Mt Victoria, there are magnificent harbour views.**

Over: CAPITAL CITY **From above the Beehive and parliament buildings this view sweeps past the commercial centre to the airport (top right).**

TRANSPORT LINKS **The only land exit from Wellington city is north along this narrow shelf shared by motorway and railway. They follow the faultline on the harbour's western side. Next to the floating dock is the terminal for the ferry service which links the North and South Islands.**

THORNDON HOUSES **The wooden Victorian residences in Wellington's oldest suburb are being rejuvenated. Many were lost during motorway construction but residents are preserving what they can of the area's unique flavour.**

SOUTH COAST, WELLINGTON **This steep and stormy seaboard takes the brunt of Cook Strait's notorious gales, providing some shelter for the city around the landlocked harbour. A track from the quarry leads to a seal colony.**

HARBOUR ENTRANCE **View from Pencarrow Head on the eastern side across to Miramar Peninsula. An inter-island ferry is about to pass the Barrett Reef, graveyard for several ships including the *Wahine* which struck it in 1968.**

CAPE TERAWHITI **The south-western extremity of the North Island. This forbidding terrain rising from Cook Strait is only a short distance from the capital.**

PAEKAKARIKI **The southern hills form into the Tararua Range and a plain begins to take shape along Wellington's western coast. Paekakariki, wedged between the two, has a gentle surf beach, which attracts many Wellingtonians in summer.**

158

OHARIU BAY **Tucked into the bay is Makara, the only beach in the rugged south-west accessible by road. There are tracks along the rocky shore.**

OLD HOUSING, PETONE **Site of New Zealand's first organised settlement, now an industrial borough.**

NEW HOUSING, TITAHI BAY **Part of Wellington's western expansion. On the far side of the entrance to Porirua Harbour is Plimmerton; the island in the distance is Kapiti.**

KAPITI COAST **Waikanae, favoured by a pleasant climate, lies between the Tararua Ranges and Kapiti Island. The island is a sanctuary for birdlife.**

MARKET GARDENS, OTAKI **The southern Manawatu Plain supports market gardens which supply most of Wellington's fruit and vegetables.**

Left: MAIN STREET, FOXTON **Foxton, the oldest town in Manawatu, once supported a thriving flax industry.**

Right: ISOLATED RESORT **View from the north towards Waikanae and the Paraparaumu Promontory. A motel has been built close to the empty beach.**

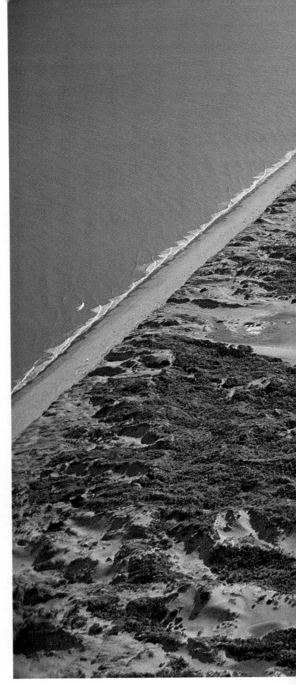

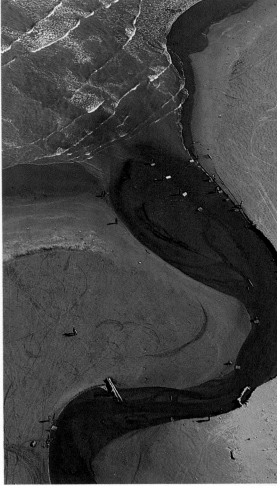

LEVIN **A** quilted pattern of market gardens spreads south of the town. A lot of fertile land has been swallowed by the expansion of Levin, a thriving farming centre that supports several light industries.

WHITEBAIT FISHING, HIMATANGI Beaches offer good surfcasting, and fish abound upriver.

SAND DUNES NEAR FOXTON **The coast has a wide strip of sand which tends to encroach on farmland. Marram grass and pines have been planted to prevent this.**

ALLUVIAL PLAIN **Rivers like the Rangitikei (here) and the Manawatu have spread alluvium from the Tararua Ranges. The resulting plains of silt loam soil are good for cropping, fat lamb production and dairying. The settlement at the Rangitikei River mouth is Tangimoana.**

163

Taranaki, King Country

The magnificent volcanic cone of Mount Egmont dominates this western coast. Its symmetrical shape, standing in isolation, can be seen from either end of the North Island. From the air, the perfect circle of Egmont's circumference is clearly discernible where the dense forest of the slopes abruptly meets the rich green pastures of the Taranaki Plains. The forested area, now protected within Egmont National Park, is one of the last remnants of the bush which once blanketed the region.

Egmont is part of a cluster of volcanoes, the older peaks of which have been weathered down and overawed by the relative newcomer. It is only two centuries since Egmont last erupted, so it cannot yet be described as extinct. Taranaki, the Maori name for the mountain, survives as the provincial title, but efforts to restore the name to the mountain have so far been unsuccessful. Captain Cook's honouring of a First Lord of the Admiralty survives.

According to Maori myth, Taranaki once belonged with the other mountains in the centre of the North Island. He wooed and won the wife of Tongariro. After a great battle involving fire, steam and hurling of rocks, Taranaki was banished to the West Coast. The path of his escape is marked by the Wanganui River.

The Wanganui was an important waterway for the Maoris and for travellers between Wellington and northern centres in early European times. The steamer service up the river was a vital link in the transport system and even after road and rail opened up the North Island, it remained popular. The beautiful river, flanked by steep bush-covered country, attracted sightseers from all over the world. In the 1930s, however, the paddle steamers were forced to end their run between Wanganui and Taumaranui because of the deterioration of the upper river. Today's tourists can still enjoy the scenery in the more mobile but less romantic jet boats.

The ranges in the upper reaches of the Wanganui River merge with the Western Uplands which meet the sea on the rugged King Country coast. This straight stretch of coastline is difficult to farm, and has no substantial settlements.

The great bulge of Taranaki's coast is quite different from the crumpled topography to the north and south. The lowlands reach out to the sea in an arc from Egmont's crater, supporting the greatest concentration of dairy farming and the most densely populated rural area in the country.

A fertile layer of volcanic ash and a high level of rainfall produce plenty of lush green grass, ideal for dairying. Most farms are small, divided by neat thorn hedges. Their regular pattern is broken by the less tidy divisions created by numerous rivers and streams which gouge their way down the sides of Mount Egmont and through the rolling pastures to the coast.

A distinctive feature of Taranaki's human settlements is the number of dairy factories. The co-operative system which is still the basis of New Zealand's dairy industry flourished in Taranaki, but many of the butter and cheese factories are now deserted. Production is becoming more centralised as small companies amalgamate in the interest of efficiency. As one moves away from the plains, either towards the north or the south, the ubiquitous cow gives way to beef cattle and sheep.

Although agriculture will continue to be the mainstay of the region's economy into the foreseeable future, new sources of wealth are being developed. Taranaki is the focus of New Zealand's energy hopes at a time when there is an urgent need to find alternatives to imported oil. In 1959, gas and condensate was discovered at Kapuni. Ten years later the much larger Maui field was discovered off shore. Condensate from the wells is shipped out from New Plymouth to the refinery at Whangarei and Kapuni natural gas is piped to Wellington and Auckland. The possible future uses of the large reserves of gas are being debated while the search for other fields continues.

Another resource which has recently been effectively exploited is the iron ore in the black sands that line the western coast. Wind and sea have spread the metal from its source in the volcanic area around Mount Egmont so that it reaches from Wanganui in the south to north of Auckland. The ore is extracted from Waipipi and Taharoa for export to Japan. Specially designed ore carriers call regularly to load the concentrate and ship it to Japanese steel mills.

Today's peaceful, prosperous rural landscape is very different from that which the traveller of a century ago would have seen. The conversion from forest to farmland came later here than in the rest of the country. The ambitions of European settlers in Taranaki and Waikato to extend their landholdings encountered strong resistance from the Maoris. The Land Wars started over the questionable purchase of the fertile plain at Waitara on the North Taranaki coast.

Although most of the Maori owners were opposed to the deal, it was enforced by government troops. For the next 20 years battles continued to flare up throughout Taranaki and Waikato.

The name King Country is a reminder of this bitter period in New Zealand's history. It derives from the Maori King movement whose followers in Waikato sought refuge in the rugged western hills during the land struggles. After peace has been made they returned and today have an impressive headquarters at Ngaruawahia on the banks of the Waikato River.

The King Country was one of the most difficult areas to convert into productive farmland. Efforts to tame it made very little headway until this century, and there is still a raw look about the bare hills. Blackened stumps and weathered logs scattered among the paddocks of grass testify to the burning and clearing that have taken place. Signs of erosion show that it has not always been successful.

Substantial areas of native forest have survived in the King Country, providing employment in logging and milling. But many of the timber towns are now disappearing. Pressure from conservation groups, aimed at preserving remaining areas of native forest, has led to major reductions in the amount of logging.

The sparseness of the population is especially apparent along the coast. North from Awakino, there are no roads or settlements at all until the long straight stretch of surf-pounded cliffs ends at the lovely Kawhia Harbour. The township of Kawhia was established by early missionaries and retains a tranquillity belonging to another era.

The next harbour, Raglan, is also very beautiful. The closest seaside resort to Hamilton, it is less remote than Kawhia but also has a quiet peaceful charm.

This section of our circumnavigation ends in the lowlands of the Waikato Basin. Although it is reminiscent of the dairy country in Taranaki, there is nothing to compare here or anywhere else with the dramatic presence of Mount Egmont.

THE EVER-PRESENT MOUNTAIN **From virtually any part of Taranaki, the imposing cone of Mount Egmont (also known as Mount Taranaki) dominates the skyline. Viewed from the southern end of the main street of Patea, the peak takes on a mystical 'hovering' quality.**

WHANGAEHU RIVER **The river snakes through the rich lowlands near Wanganui at the end of its run from Mount Ruapehu in the centre of the North Island.**

WANGANUI **Its position at the mouth of the Wanganui River gave it an importance in Maori and early European times as a link between other coastal centres and the interior. Since the decline of its river port, Wanganui has become a slow growing provincial market town with some secondary industry.**

RELIGIOUS COMMUNITY **Ratana owes its name and its existence to W. T. Ratana, founder of the largest distinctively Maori religion. In the 1920s he rapidly built a reputation as a seer and faithhealer; thousands flocked to him to be cured or to meet 'the Mouthpiece of God'. The movement took on social and political dimensions and became separated from the main Protestant churches.**

SOUTH TARANAKI FARMLAND **A prime reason for the concentration of dairying in Taranaki is that its climate encourages good grass growth. Mount Egmont strongly influences that climate by directing moist winds up and around itself, producing an evenly distributed rainfall.**

167

ENERGY WEALTH **Kapuni gas is treated after being brought to the surface in South Taranaki and then piped to Auckland and Wellington as natural gas for domestic and industrial use.**

Above: FUTURE PROSPECTS **The much larger Maui field off the Taranaki coast will reduce New Zealand's dependence on imported oil. This major resource is likely to produce liquid petroleum gas, compressed natural gas and methanol.**

Left: SOUTH TARANAKI COAST **View from near Patea, before the coastline curves outwards.**

EGMONT SUMMIT **The 2518-metre-high peak is a popular target for climbers. Although it is not difficult to scale in summer, weather conditions can change suddenly and many lives have been lost here.**

CHEESE COUNTRY The crumpled land surface is a legacy of the lava and mud flows on the western side of the Taranaki volcanoes, near Okato. The soil is not particularly fertile and requires constant applications of fertiliser to support the cheese production for which this area is famous.

GUNFIGHTERS PA **This serrated trench at Whenua-kura was probably built during the Land Wars last century. Traditional Maori fortifications were adapted to suit the newly acquired guns.**

Above: SEA SCULPTURES **The edge of the South Taranaki plain.**

Over: EGMONT NATIONAL PARK **The dark green skirt of the park surrounds Mount Egmont and the older volcanic peaks to the north.**

171

DORMANT VOLCANO **Mount Egmont is the most westerly in the line of volcanoes through the centre of the North Island. Unlike Ngauruhoe, Ruapehu and Tongariro, it is no longer active. Egmont last erupted about 200 years ago.**

NATURAL WEALTH **Lush green dairy pastures contrast strikingly with the black sandy beach at Omata west of New Plymouth. Further south at Waipipi, iron ore is extracted from the black sands and the concentrate is sent to Japan in specially designed ships.**

FISHING VILLAGE **These cottages make up a small fishing village on the north Taranaki coast. There are several such settlements situated on river mouths along this stretch of coastline. Despite its remote location, the town's layout is rigidly neat. Variations in pastel coloured house paint provide the only glimmers of individuality.**

SCULPTED LANDSCAPE **At Tongaporutu the coastline changes abruptly from the jagged white cliffs around Paraninihi to a lower tableland edged in smooth sandstone. Over thousands of years, the waves have carved the cliff faces into impressive shapes and created huge caves. In one of these, behind the ocean beach, early Maori rock drawings have been discovered.**

MAORI LANDMARK **The white cliffs of Paraninihi (seen here from Tongaporutu). Tongaporutu marked the territorial dividing line between the Maoris of Waikato and Taranaki. The only way to pass between the two areas was to swing across on a vine rope. In the 1850s, the Attorney-General had to walk back to Auckland after a hostile warrior refused him passage.**

A LIFE OF EASE **The Taranaki area, renowned for its prosperous dairying industry, was the site of New Zealand's first dairying co-operative.**

TEA ROOMS **A typical style of timber building houses the tea rooms at Patea. Hospitality is offered with the refreshments by the Maori family who operate the business.**

Above: PLANT NURSERY NEAR WAITARA **Ornamental trees and shrubs grown on some of Taranaki's richest soil are supplied to gardeners throughout New Zealand. This nursery also ships plants overseas.**

Over: TONGAPORUTU **A boiling sea attacks the cliffs along this spectacular stretch of coastline.**

TE MAIKA, KAWHIA HARBOUR An isolated settlement on the southern side of the entrance to lovely Kawhia Harbour. Further south, over the hills in the distance, Taharoa's isolation has been ended by the trade with Japan in ore from its black ironsands.

Right: WAIKATO RIVER DELTA The Waikato, New Zealand's longest river, fans out as it approaches the Tasman Sea south of Auckland. Most of the electric power that supplies the North Island is generated from hydro-electric stations that have been built on the Waikato River.

The North

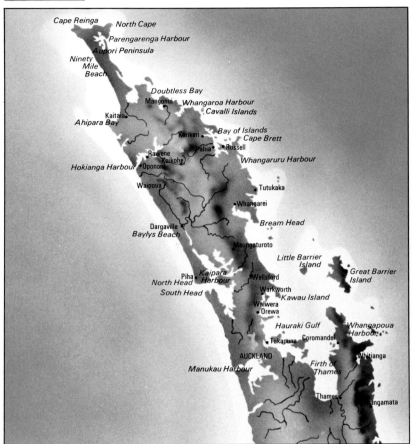

From Auckland to North Cape the coast is the dominant aspect of the landscape. This most fascinating part of New Zealand is nearly all coast — one long narrow peninsula packed with variety and contrast. The east and west, separated by so little land, are completely different. The Maoris interpreted it as the difference between the savage male and the gentle female. The western, or male, coast is pounded by the Tasman Sea, propelled in by the force of the predominant wind. It has created a seemingly endless stretch of dark sand in a line broken only by the harbours of Manukau, Kaipara and Hokianga, each with a treacherous sand bar at its entrance. The east side by comparison has an indented coast of sheltered bays, tranquil coves, peninsulas, islands and alluring white sand beaches.

There are also marked contrasts in the population density of the region. Auckland has New Zealand's greatest concentration of people while the Far North and Coromandel are sparsely populated. Historically, the warm northern climate has always attracted more settlement than in other parts of the country. The first Polynesian arrivals would have found the conditions closer to what they were accustomed to, and most Maoris lived here as they still do. European beginnings were concentrated on the Bay of Islands which saw the first missionary efforts and the start of colonial government. Europeans also exploited the North's resources of whales, kauri gum and timber, and gold. The city of Auckland, slow to get started, has had remarkable growth this century at the expense of southern centres.

The neck is almost severed from the main body of the North Island where the Manukau Harbour bites in from the west, nearly reaching the eastern Waitemata Harbour. Between the two lies the city of Auckland among dozens of volcanic cones and craters. The urban area now spreads to such an extent north and south of the isthmus that it is difficult to define where Auckland begins and ends. It is a city built around the car. Motorways from south and west slash through the city until they meet in a huge concrete knot and then continue in a highway across the Harbour Bridge to the North Shore. Whole new cities have developed along the northern beaches; Auckland was not planned, it has grown haphazardly and rapidly.

Those who have come to the metropolis include Pacific Islanders and rural Maoris. The strong Polynesian influence is part of Auckland's distinctive character. Many volcanic cones display striking evidence of the earlier Maori occupation of the site. They were laboriously terraced to create fortified villages (pas); in fact, there are similar pa sites on hills and headlands throughout the north.

Auckland's semi tropical climate is primarily what sets it apart from the other cities and draws people to it; the climate, and the superb beaches and waterways. Auckland's way of life is casual and outdoor oriented. There are no extremes of weather apart from high humidity in summer. Rainfall is also high but generally comes in showers and does not interfere much with the outdoor lifestyle. Yachting and boating are popular; the Waitemata and the Gulf beyond offer one of the finest stretches of water for sailing in the world.

The Hauraki Gulf between the mainland and the protective ridge of the Coromandel Peninsula, has over a hundred islands of varying sizes. The closest to Auckland, and the city's symbol, is Rangitoto. This newest and most perfectly shaped volcano erupted from the sea within the last 1000 years. Of the other islands within the Gulf, Waiheke is the largest and supports a substantial permanent population. The more distant islands are refuges for bird and plant life. Many different seabirds and some of New Zealand's rarest native birds nest on their protected rocks and trees. Little Barrier Island is the only place in the country where the vegetation has not been disturbed by introduced browsing animals. Beneath the clear waters of the Gulf the rich marine life beckons the underwater diver.

The Coromandel is within sight of Auckland but is a world apart. Both were forged in the same period of volcanic activity but in subsequent earth movement the Coromandel ridge was thrust upwards as the land block to the west sank below sea level to become the Firth of Thames. The Coromandel hills have been gouged by erosion since their forest cover was plundered last century to extract kauri timber for use in British shipyards. Human activity reached its height after the discovery of gold in the mid 1800s. The towns of Coromandel, Thames and Waihi sprang up near the main finds. In 1870 Thames had a population three times its present size. Recently there has been renewed interest in mining in the area, but it is best known as a holiday place, especially along the beaches and bays of the Pacific coast.

The approach to Northland from Auckland passes pohutukawa lined golden beaches, crowded in summer. Some of the choicest areas have been saved from the destructive forces of development through the far sighted policy of the Auckland Regional Authority who have established coastal parks. Particularly attractive is the reserved land bordering the outlet of the Mahurangi River. It leads to the picturesque town of Warkworth which, like most northern settlements, relied on sea transport until comparatively recently.

The ragged eastern coast smooths out in a double sweep before reaching Whangarei Harbour, site of the Marsden Point oil refinery. After it was built in the 1960s, the port and city of Whangarei developed rapidly. The centre of Northland, it supports one third of the region's population. Missionaries paved the way for settlement here, where British sovereignty was proclaimed in 1840.

The only other significant port in Northland is in the Bay of Islands where the main industry is tourism. The natural beauty and rich historical associations have been saved by a century of neglect after the initial flurry of European activity.

A short distance across to the west coast, Hokianga Harbour is also haunted by the past, but its memories are undisturbed by invasions of fleeting tourists. New Zealand's first industry, shipbuilding, started in this harbour surrounded by kauri timber. In less than a century the magnificent forests had all but gone. The Kaipara and Hokianga harbours, bustling ports while the timber industry flourished, gave up their denuded shores to farmers and their silted waters to recreational boaters.

The west coast becomes emptier and lonelier the further north it stretches. The sandy finger of Ninety Mile Beach, reaching out to the volcanic tips of Cape Reinga and North Cape, feels like the end of the world. According to Maori legend, it was. They believed that where the oceans meet, the spirits of the dead went to the other world.

OPITO BAY, COROMANDEL **A typical northern beach, it has a sandy sheltered shore and gentle surf. The development of holiday subdivisions has reduced this coast's isolation.**

TAIRUA HARBOUR **Paku Hill, an early Maori pa site, keeps watch over the harbour where sailing vessels used to load their cargoes of timber. The area is a popular holiday destination for Aucklanders. Pauanui on the far side is a carefully planned replica of suburban life complete with golf course.**

Left: EAST COROMANDEL COAST **The turbulent seas along this coastline have carved spectacular shapes in the limestone foreshore near Hahei.**

Above: COROMANDEL SEASCAPE **Mahurangi Island, viewed through limestone formations at Cathedral Cave, Hahei. This coastline has many islands.**

COROMANDEL TOWNSHIP **Some of the drowned hills of its harbour rise in the distance. Coromandel takes its name from a British naval ship which came here in 1820 to load kauri spars. Thirty-two years later gold was discovered nearby and the town came into being.**

LIVING HISTORY **Coromandel has the air of a nineteenth century frontier town. Many wooden buildings erected during the mining boom are still in use.**

WHANGAPOUA STATE FOREST **Coromandel's steep terrain is more suited to forestry than grazing. Exotic pines have taken the place of the noble kauri.**

MINERAL WEALTH **The outlet of Waiaro stream on Coromandel's west coast. The peninsula yields New Zealand's richest concentration of minerals.**

THAMES **The gold rush town of last century is much smaller today, although there has been renewed mining activity in recent years.**

TRAM BACH **When Auckland scrapped its trams in 1956 many were converted into unusual holiday homes on the coast north of Thames.**

185

YACHTSMAN'S PARADISE **Auckland has a very high concentration of boat owners. The Waitemata Harbour and Hauraki Gulf are ideally suited to yachting. These yachts are racing through the Rangitoto Channel towards the Gulf, leaving the harbour and city in the distance.**

GANNET COLONY **Tirikohua Point on Auckland's west coast. On the rock pillar below the nesting place a lone fisherman tries his luck.**

CAPE COLVILLE **The northern tip of Coromandel Peninsula, it flanks the crescent shaped beach of Port Jackson. Great Barrier Island, on the horizon, was originally joined to the peninsula. The waterway which now separates them, Colville Channel, carries most of the shipping into the port of Auckland.**

PAKIRI BEACH **Between the northern end of Hauraki Gulf and Whangarei, the east coast's ragged line smooths out into an exposed ocean beach, which is one of the beauty spots of the area.**

AUCKLAND SUMMER **The attraction of Auckland lies in its mild climate and the number and variety of its beaches. This is Murrays Bay on the North Shore, a popular spot for yachtsmen and swimmers.** *Photograph:* **Robin Smith.**

Left: AUCKLAND **From above the commercial centre of New Zealand's largest city, looking north across the Waitemata Harbour towards Devonport and the perfect cone of Rangitoto. A line of high-rise buildings running up from the port marks Queen Street, the city's main thoroughfare. Nestled in the trees to the right is Old Government House, built in the brief period before 1865 when Auckland was the capital.**

Over: SOUTH HEAD, KAIPARA HARBOUR **Dunes of light coloured sand take over from the black volcanic sand of Auckland's western beaches. Kaipara, New Zealand's largest harbour, has myriad mangrove fringed inlets clawing almost to the east coast. Its tranquil waters become treacherous at the harbour entrance.**

MAHURANGI HEADS These bush-covered headlands near the mouth of the Mahurangi River and adjacent to the Wenderholm Reserve form part of the Auckland Regional Authority's network of coastal parks.

HAURAKI GULF **The pohutukawa-lined Wenderholm Reserve looks out to the islands of the Hauraki Gulf, a rich recreational resource for the maritime city of Auckland.**

KOLA DANCERS, DARGAVILLE **The girls are descendants of the many Yugoslavs who emigrated around 1900 to work in the gumfields of the North.**

Above: KAURI SAWMILL, WHANGAROA HARBOUR **The few logs still available are kept for specialist use such as boat building and furniture making.**

Right: KAURI **Milling during the nineteenth century destroyed all but a few remnants of the unique kauri forests which are now protected reserves.**

HOKIANGA HARBOUR ENTRANCE **From the holiday resort of Omapere the narrow harbour winds inland, forming numerous arms and inlets.**

Left: WEST COAST NORTH OF KAIPARA **Maunganui Bluff is one of the few promontories to break the long, lonely line of wild beaches stretching north.**

MANGROVES **Vegetation like this, beside the Whirinaki River, is found only on tidal mudflats north of Waikato.**

MORNING MIST, BAY OF ISLANDS **This most beautiful and historic bay was formed when the sea drowned the valley floors and turned the hills into islands.**

TERRACED PA, BLAND BAY **Maori settlements such as this no longer need protection from outside attackers. The symmetrically shaped pa remains only as an historic reminder. The township is situated on an isthmus between the Pacific Ocean and Whangaruru Harbour.**

HOKIANGA CHURCH **Elevated churches, like this one at Matawhera, survey the rolling country where missionaries were active as early as the 1820s.**

CAPE BRETT **The entrance to the Bay of Islands is guarded by a lighthouse. The tall island, called Piercy, is known for its 'Hole in the Rock', an archway big enough for tourist launches to travel through. The surrounding waters have also achieved fame as a sportsground for big game fishermen.**

CITRUS ORCHARDS, KERIKERI The volcanic soil and benevolent climate of this pleasant area make it one of the richest pockets in the country, popular with people retiring from the cities. The land was subdivided for citrus growing in the 1920s, a century after it became the first soil in New Zealand to be ploughed. In the picturesque Kerikeri Basin, the buildings and atmosphere of the oldest surviving mission settlement have been preserved.

OPUA, BAY OF ISLANDS **Opua is the second major port of Northland after Whangarei. It is the base for a vehicular ferry connecting the main towns of the bay with New Zealand's first town, Russell.**

Right: WAITANGI, BIRTHPLACE OF THE NATION **In 1840, Maori chiefs signed the Treaty of Waitangi outside the British resident's house. The flagpole is the centrepiece of a ceremony on 6 February every year.**

GUMFIELDS, AHIPARA **Scars left by gumdiggers on the last major gumfield, a barren plateau above Ninety Mile Beach. Fossilised kauri resin, used to make varnishes and linoleum, was extracted by hordes of diggers camped here in the 1930s.**

DOUBTLESS BAY **A Maori pa site sits at one end of Coopers Beach. Nearby at Taipa is the supposed landing place of Kupe, the legendary first discoverer of New Zealand. Taipa and Coopers Beach are two of the most northerly beaches to attract large numbers of holiday makers.**

Left: HOROROA POINT **On the jagged coastline between Whangaroa Harbour and Matauri Bay, this unspoilt area offers superb beaches, spectacular scenery and splendid fishing. Captain Cook named the offshore islands Cavalli after the fish supplied by local Maoris (probably trevally).**

PIPIS **A 'kit' (basket) full, gathered from the sand at the low tide mark. Shellfish were a major part of coastal dwelling Maoris' diets.**

NINETY MILE BEACH **The long, narrow sand strip links North Cape and Cape Reinga to the mainland. The beach is actually 90 kilometres long.**

Left: AWANUI RIVER **This Far North river empties into Rangaunu Harbour, an almost landlocked shallow basin which opens into Rangaunu Bay.**

CAPE REINGA **The northern tip, legendary departure point of the spirits. Cape Maria van Diemen is on the western horizon.**

Index

Abel Tasman	10, 94, 112	Cape Reinga	180, 203	Falls, Thundercreek	29
Abel Tasman National Park	94, 109, 112	Cape Runaway	114, 122, 123	Farewell Spit	94, 113
Acheron	30	Cape Terawhiti	158	Fiord, Middle	30
Admiralty Bay	105	Cape Turakirae	132, 151	Fiord, South	30
Ahipara	201	Cape Turnagain	132, 142	Fiordland	10, 30-47
Akaroa	81	Caroline Bay	77	Fiordland National Park	30, 42
Akaroa Harbour	70, 81	Cascade Cove	44	Firth of Thames	8, 180
Alexandra	61	Cascade Point	30, 32	Flaxbourne	94
Alpine Fault	96	Castlepoint	132, 145	Fortrose	55
Alpine Range	10, 70	Castor Bay	189	Fossil Forest, Curio Bay	55
Alps, Southern	8	Caswell Sound	30	Foulwind, Cape	10, 17
Amanita muscaria	87	Cathedral Cave, Hahei	183	Four Peaks Range	8, 81-82
Aorangi Mountains	146	Catlins River	58	Fourteen Mile Bluff	15-16
Arahura River	10	Catlins State Forest Park	48	Foveaux Strait	46, 48, 52
Arahura Valley	19	Catlins Wilderness	54, 55	Fox Glacier	10, 20, 24, 25
Aramoana, Wairarapa Coast	141	Central Otago	48	Foxton	152, 160, 163
Arapawa Island	99	Charles Sound	30, 38	Franz Josef Glacier	10, 20, 21, 24, 25
Arawata Bill	30	Charleston	16	Franz Josef Neve	21
Arawata River	30	Chasland, Tommy	55	French Pass Settlement	103
Aropaoanui	134	Cheviot Estate	90		
Ashburton	77, 80-82	Christ's College, Christchurch	85	**Gable End Foreland**	131
Aspiring, Mount	63	Christ Church Cathedral, Nelson	106	Gabriel's Gully	62
Atawhai	106	Christchurch	70, 77, 83	George Sound	30, 37
Auckland	152, 164, 169, 180, 186, 189	Clarence River	94, 96	Geraldine	81-82
Avon River	70	Clifton	82	Geraldine Downs	8
Awakino	164	Clinton Canyon	36	Gibb, Peter	108
Awanui River	203	Clinton Valley	30	Gisborne	114, 125, 131
Awatare River	98, 99	Clutha River	48, 54, 58, 61, 63	Glendhu Bay	63
		'Coaster', the	10	Glover, Denis	30
Balclutha	58	Collingwood	94	Golden Bay	12, 94, 112
Banks, Sir Joseph	125	Colville, Cape	187	Gore Bay	91
Banks Peninsula	70, 81, 82	Colville Channel	187	Grampian Mountains	73
Barrett Reef	152, 157	Conical Hill	8	Granity	14
Bay of Islands	196, 197, 180	Cook, Captain James	10, 17, 30,	Grassmere, Lake	94, 96
Bay of Plenty, East Cape	114-131		39, 44-46, 94, 103, 114, 123, 125,	Greigs Settlement	18
Ben Ohau Range	73		138, 142, 164, 201	Grenadier Rocks	13
Benmore, Lake	74	Cook, Mount	17, 39, 73	Grey River	10
Birchfield	14	Cook Strait	94, 96, 103, 146,	Greymouth	10, 17
Black Head	65		152, 157, 158	Grigg, John	80
Blackhead	141	Cook's Cove, Tolaga Bay	114, 125		
Bland Bay	196	Coopers Beach	201	**Haast**	32
Blenheim	94, 98	Coromandel	180, 184	Haast River	29, 30
Bligh Sound	30	Coromandel Coast	183	Haast Valley	29
Bluff	48	Coromandel Peninsula	8, 114, 180, 187	Hagley Park, Christchurch	82, 83
Bluff Harbour	51, 52	Croisilles Harbour	105	Hahei	183
Bluff Hill	52	Cromwell Gorge	61	Hakateramea River	74
Botanic Gardens, Christchurch	85	Culverdon, North Canterbury	87	Half Moon Bay	51
Boulder Bank, Nelson Haven	106	Curio Bay Fossil Forest	55	Hall Range	74
Bowen Falls	35			Hamilton	164
Brain Pot, Rotorua	118	**Dalgety Range**	73	Hanmer Springs	8
Breaksea Island	45	Dargaville	193	Hanmer Springs Forest	87
Breaksea Sound	45	Darran Mountains	30	Hastings	132, 138
Brett, Cape	197	Deep Cove	30	Hawaki Gulf	180, 186, 189, 193
Brightwater	108	Denniston Incline	15	Haurangi Forest Park	146
Brothers Point	54	Devonport	189	Hautaki	99
Bruce Bay	16, 25, 29	Doubtful Sound	30, 39, 44	Hawea Lake	48
Buller	10	Doubtless Bay	201	Hawea River	63
Buller River	10	Dual Bridge, Seddon	98	Hawke Bay	132, 134, 135, 138
		Dunedin	48, 64	Hawkes Bay, Wairarapa	132-151
Campbell, Cape	94, 96	D'Urville Island	103, 105	Heaphy River	10, 12
Canterbury	48, 70-93, 132	Dusky Sound	30, 44, 46	Heaphy Track	12
Canterbury, North	52, 70			Heathcote River	70, 84
Canterbury Plain	70, 81, 82	**Eastbourne**	152	Heretaunga Plains	132, 138
Canterbury, South	80	East Cape, Bay of Plenty	114-131	Himatangi	162
Cape Campbell	94, 96	East Island	125	Hinds River	80
Cape Brett	197	Egmont, Mount	164, 167, 169	Hokianga Harbour	180, 195
Cape Colville	187	Egmont National Park	164, 171	Hokitika	10, 18, 19
Cape Foulwind	10, 17	*Endeavour*	30, 94, 103, 131, 132	Hollyford River	35
Cape Kidnappers	132, 138, 140	Endeavour Inlet	103	Hororoa Beach	201
Cape Maria van Diemen	203			Hunt Beach	25
Cape, North	203	**Falls Bowen**	35	Huriawa Peninsula	66
Cape Palliser	132, 150	Falls, Sutherland	30, 36	Hurunui River	91

Hutt, Lower 152
Hutt River 152
Hutt, Upper 152

Ianthe Forest 19
Ikawhenua Range 114
Inchclutha Island 48, 58
Inland Kaikoura Ranges 96
Invercargill 48, 51
Isobel, Mount 8
Isobel, Mount Ranges 8

Jackson Bay 30, 32
Jackson Head 30
Jones, Johnny 66

Kaiapohia Peninsula 70
Kaiapoi 70
Kaikoura 70, 90, 93
Kaikoura Coast 94, 96
Kaikoura Lowlands 94
Kaikoura Peninsula 70, 92
Kaikoura Ranges 70, 114
Kaipara 195
Kaipara Harbour 180, 189
Kaitangata 58
Kaiteriteri 94
Kakanui 68
Kapiti Coast 152, 160
Kapiti Island 160
Kapuni 164
Karamea 10, 12, 13
Karangarua River 25
Karitane 66
Karitane Beach 48
Kawhia 164
Kawhia Harbour 178
Kekerengu 96
Kenepuru Sound 94
Kepler Range 42
Kerikeri 198
Kidnappers, Cape 132, 138, 140
King Country, Taranaki 164-179
King, Sir Truby 66
Kirkilston Range 73, 74
Kupe 201

Lake Benmore 74
Lake Grassmere 94, 96
Lake Hawea 48
Lake McKerrow 35
Lake Manapouri 30, 42, 44, 48
Lake Ohau 70, 73
Lake Pukaki 70, 73
Lake Quill 36
Lake Rotomahana 118
Lake Taupo 114
Lake Te Anau 30, 42
Lake Tekapo 70, 73
Lake Wairarapa 132, 151
Lake Wanaka 48, 63
Larnach Castle 66
Larnach, W.J. 66
Lawrence 8, 48, 62
Levin 152, 162
Little Barrier Island 180
Little Wanganui 12
Longbeach Homestead 80
Lower Hutt 152
Lyttelton 70, 83, 152
Lyttelton Harbour 70, 81

Mackenzie Basin 73
Mackenzie Country 73, 74
McKerrow, Lake 35
Mackinnon Pass 30, 36
Mahia Peninsula 132. 135
Mahurangi Heads 192
Mahurangi Island 183
Mahurangi River 180, 192
Main Divide 44, 70
Makara 152, 159
Makawhio Point 25
Mana Island 159
Manakau Harbour 180
Manapouri, Lake 30, 42, 44, 48
Manapouri Village 44
Manawatu, Wellington 152-163
Manawatu Gorge 152
Manawatu Plain 160
Manawatu River 152, 163
Maria van Diemen, Cape 203
Malborough, Nelson 94-113
Malborough Sounds 94, 103
Martins Bay 30, 35
Masterton 132, 145
Matahiwi 138
Matanaka 66
Matakana Island 114
Matata 119
Mataura River 54, 55
Matauri Bay 201
Matawhera 196
Matiri Range 12
Maui 164, 169
Maunganui Bluff 195
Maunganui, Mount 114, 117
Mayor Island 114
Middle Fiord 30
Milford Sound 30, 35, 37
Milford Track 35
Miramar Peninsula 157
Mitre Peak 30
Moeraki 29
Moeraki Beach 48
Motunau River 86
Moeraki Boulders, North Otago 68
Motu River 121
Motunau 91
Motunau Beach 86
Mount Aspiring 63
Mount Aspriring National Park 63
Mount Cook 17, 39, 73
Mount Egmont 164, 167, 169, 174
Mount Isobel Ranges 8
Mount Maunganui 114, 117
Mount Ngauruhoe 174
Mount Peel Range 81-82
Mount Ruapehu 166, 174
Mount Tarawera 117, 118
Mount Tasman 17
Mount Tongariro 174
Mount Victoria 152
Murchison Mountains 30, 42
Murderers Bay 94
Muttonbird Islands 53

Nancy Sound 30
Napier 132, 135
Neck, The 53
Nelson 94, 106
Nelson Haven 106
New Plymouth 164, 174
Ngakawau 15

Ngaruroro, River 132
Ngaruwahia 164
Ngauruhoe, Mount 174
Ngawihi 146
Ninety Mile Beach 180, 201, 203
North Canterbury 52, 70
North Canterbury Ranges 86
North Cape 180, 203
North Otago 48
North, the 180-203
Northwest Nelson Forest Park 12

Oamaru 48, 68, 69
Oban 51
Ocean Beach 132
Oharu Bay 159
Ohau, Lake 70, 73
Ohope 114
Okarito Lagoon 20
Okato 170
Okuru River 32
Omapere 195
Omata 174
Opito Bay 180
Opotiki 114
Opua, Bay of Islands 199
Orbell, Dr Geoffrey 30
Otago 30
Otago, Central 48
Otago Harbour 65
Otago Peninsula 65
Otago, South 48
Otago, Southland 48-69
Otago University 48
Otaki 152, 160
Otakou Marae 66
Owhiro Bay 152

Paekakariki 152, 158
Pakiri Beach 189
Paku Hill 183
Palliser Bay 132, 146, 151
Palliser, Cape 132, 150
Palmerston North 152
Pancake Rocks 10, 15-16
Paparoa Range 15-17
Paraninihi 175
Paraparaumu 152
Paraparaumu Promontory 160
Parititahi Tunnel, Kaikowa 90
Patea 164, 169, 175
Paterson Inlet 48, 53
Pauanui 183
Pegasus Bay 70
Pelorus Sound 94, 103, 105
Pencarrow 152
Pencarrow Head 157
Petone 152, 159
Picton 94, 152
Picton Harbour 103
Piercy Island 197
Pigeon Bay 81
Plimmerton 159
Porangahau River 141
Porirua Harbour 152, 159
Port Chalmers 65
Port Hills 82
Port Nelson 106
Poverty Bay 114, 131, 132, 142
Preservation Inlet 30, 46
Public Hospital, Christchurch 85
Pukaki, Lake 70, 73

Punakaiki 10
Putangirua Pinnacles 150
Puysegur Point 46

Queen Charlotte Sound 94, 103
Queens Park 51
Quill, Lake 36

Raglan 164
Rakaia River 77
Rangauna Bay 203
Rangauna Harbour 203
Rangitaiki Plains 114
Rangitikei River 163
Rangitoto 189
Rangitoto Channel 186
Rangitoto Island 180
Ratana 167
Ratana, W.T 167
Raukumara Range 114, 121
Reinga, Cape 180, 203
Resolution 30, 44
Rhodes brothers 81
Rimutaka Hill 152
Rimutaka Range 132
River, Arahura 10
River, Arawata 30
River, Avon 70, 84, 85
River, Awanui 203
River, Awatare 98, 99
River, Buller 10
River, Catlins 58
River, Clarence 94, 96
River, Clutha 48, 54, 58, 61, 63
River, Grey 10
River, Haast 29, 30
River, Hakateramea 74
River, Hawea 63
River, Heaphy 10, 12
River, Heathcote 70, 84
River, Hinds 80
River, Hollyford 35
River, Hurunui 91
River, Hutt 152
River, Karangarua 25
River, Mahurangi 180, 192
River, Manawatu 152, 163
River, Mataura 54, 55
River, Motu 121
River, Motunau 86
River, Ngaruroro 132
River, Okuru 32
River, Porangahau 141
River, Rangitikei 163
River, Ruamahanga 151
River Taramakau 10, 18
River Tukituki 132, 141
River, Tutaekuri 132
River, Waiho 20, 24
River, Waikato 164, 178
River, Waimarie 13
River Wairaurahiri 46
River, Wanganui 164
River, Whangaehu 166
River, Whareama 145
River, Whirinaki 195
Riversdale 132, 145
Riverton 48
Riwaka 108
Rotomahana, Lake 118
Rotorua 114, 118
Roxburgh 48

Roxburgh Dam 62
Ruahine Range 141
Ruamahanga River 151
Ruamahanga Valley 132, 151
Ruapehu, Mount 166, 174
Ruapuke Island 52
Ruby Beach 35
Runaway, Cape 114, 122, 123
Russell 199

Sails of Kupe, Palliser Bay 147
St Clair 65
Sandfly Point 30
Seal Islands 46
Seaward Kaikoura Range 90, 92, 96
Seddon 98
Seymour Square, Blenheim 98
Ship Cove 94, 103
South Brighton 70, 84
South Canterbury 80
South Fiord 30
South Island Mountains 46
South Taranaki 169
South Taranaki Plain 171
South Westland State Forest 29
Southern Alps 8, 10, 29, 39, 70, 73, 74
Southland, Otago 48-69
Stockton 10, 15
Stephens Island 105
Stewart Island 51, 53
Sumner 82
Sumner Head 82
Sumner's Cave Rock 84
Sutherland Falls 30, 36

Taharoa 164, 178
Tahunanui 94
Taipa 201
Tairua Harbour 183
Takahe Valley 30, 42
Takitumu 132
Tangimoana 163
Taramakau River 10, 18
Taranaki, King Country 164-179
Taranaki Plains 164
Taranaki Volcanoes 170
Tararua 48, 54
Tararua Ranges 158, 160
Tarawera, Mount 117, 118
Tasman, Abel 10, 94, 112
Tasman Bay 94, 105, 109
Tasman, Mount 17
Tasman Sea 10, 12, 24, 178
Tata Beach 112
Tata Islands 94, 112
Tatapouri 131
Taumaranui 164
Taupo, Lake 114
Tauranga 114
Tauranga Harbour 114, 117
Tawhitinui Reach 105
Taylors Mistake 82
Te Anau 30, 39, 42
Te Anau, Lake 30, 42
Te Kaha 118, 122
Tekapo 74
Tekapo, Lake 70, 73
Te Maiko, Kawhia Harbour 178
Te Rauparaha 70, 152
Terawhiti, Cape 158
Te Waewae Bay 48, 51
Thames 180, 185

Thames, Firth of 8
Thompson Sound 30
Thorndon, Wellington 157
Thundercreek Falls 29
Timaru 70, 77
Timaru Downs 81
Timaru Harbour 77
Tirikohua Point 186
Tiromoana 17
Titahi Bay 159
Tiwai Point 48, 51, 52
Toetoes Harbour 55
Toitoi 55
Tolaga Bay 125
Tongaporutu 175
Tongariro 164
Tongariro, Mount 174
Torrent Bay 112
Tory Channel 94, 99
Totaranui 109
Troup, G. 65
Tuhawaiki 52
Tuhawaiki Point 77
Tukituki River 132, 141
Turakirae, Cape 132, 151
Turnagain, Cape 132, 142
Tutaekuri River 132
Twelve Mile Bluff 15-16

University of Canterbury, Old 85
University, Otago 48
Upper Hutt 152

Victoria, Mount 152
Volcanic Plateau 114

Wahine 152, 157
Waiaro Stream 185
Waiau Bluffs 90
Waiau River 48
Waiheke Island 180
Waihi 180
Wahio River 20, 24
Waikanae 152, 160
Waikato 164, 195
Waikato Basin 164
Waikato River 164, 178
Waikawau 8
Waikawa Harbour 54
Waikouaiti Bay 66
Waikouaiti Beach 48
Waimakariri River 70
Waimarama Beach 132
Waimarie River 13
Waimea Inlet 106
Wainomo Lagoon 77
Waipapa Point 54
Waipara 70
Waipara River 91
Waipipi 164, 174
Waipipi Point 48
Wairarapa, Hawkes Bay 132-151
Wairarapa, Lake 132, 151
Wairau Bar 98
Wairau River 94, 99
Wairaurahiri River 46
Wairoa 132, 135
Waitaki 77
Waitaki River 48, 70, 73
Waitangi 199
Waitara 164, 175
Waitemata Harbour 180, 186, 189

Waituna Creek   *53*
Waituna Lagoon   *52, 53*
Wakatipu   48
Wakefield Settlement   70
Wanaka, Lake   48, *63*
Wanganui   152, 164, *166*
Wanganui, Little   *12*
Wanganui River   164
Warkworth   180
Warrington Beach   48
Wattie, Sir James   132
Wellington   94, *103*, 132, *145*, 164, *169*
Wellington, Manawatu   152-163
Wenderholm Reserve   *192, 193*
West Arm, Manapouri   *44*
West Coast   10-29
West Wairarapa Fault   *96*
Western Sounds   *105*
Westland   *25,* 30
Westland National Park   10, *20*
Westport   10, *15-16*
Whakaki Lagoon   *135*
Whakarewarewa   *118*
Whakatane   114
Whangaehu Cliffs, Wairarapa   *142*
Whangaehu River   *166*
Whangapoua State Forest   *185*
Whangarei   164, 180, *189,*
Whangaroa Harbour   180, *193, 201*
Whangaruru Harbour   *196*
Whareama River   *145*
Wharekura Point   *122*
Whatarangi   *146*
Whenuakura   *171*
Whirinaki River   *195*
White Island   114, *117*
Woodford House, Hawkes Bay   *138*

Young, Nicholas   *131*
Young Nicks Head   *131*